PROLEGOMENA
TO
A NEW METAPHYSIC

T0382173

PROLEGOMENA
TO
A NEW METAPHYSIC

by

Thomas Whittaker

Author of *The Neo-Platonists*

CAMBRIDGE

AT THE UNIVERSITY PRESS

MCMXXXI

CAMBRIDGE
UNIVERSITY PRESS

University Printing House, Cambridge CB2 8BS, United Kingdom

Cambridge University Press is part of the University of Cambridge.

It furthers the University's mission by disseminating knowledge in the pursuit of education, learning and research at the highest international levels of excellence.

www.cambridge.org
Information on this title: www.cambridge.org/9781107438170

First published 1931
First paperback edition 2014

A catalogue record for this publication is available from the British Library

ISBN 978-1-107-43817-0 Paperback

CONTENTS

L'illimité se refuse et s'offre à la fois, fermé à l'expérimentation, ouvert à la conjecture.

VICTOR HUGO, "Les Travailleurs de la Mer",
deuxième partie, livre deuxième, v.

I

IS THERE THEORETIC TRUTH?

IN LOOKING over recently a series of essays (not yet collected) which have all some reference to the branch of philosophy called Theory of Knowledge, I became aware retrospectively that they have a negative as well as a positive character in common. The positive character[1] is the dominating conviction that the controversy between the principles of Reason and Experience has been brought historically to an approximate solution. The negative character is that, without consciously willing the exclusion, I have never found occasion to discuss the attitude of any thinker expounded, or even incidentally cited, to the doctrine called pragmatism, now acclaimed, by the most vocal portion of the world of culture, as triumphant over the whole past thought of the human race.

Pragmatism, as I understand from its latest expositors, holds that all knowledge is essentially

[1] Especially marked in the article on "Reason" contributed to the *Encyclopaedia of Religion and Ethics* (1918).

directed to practical ends, is in short a mode of business (πράγματα). Truth is simply one kind of "biological value"—a belief which it is useful to hold for self-conservation or social conservation in the life of action. The views stated by the pragmatists, however, are so mixed with older points of view that I was once led to suggest that they have reintroduced, against the austerer theory of Baconian induction, which demands immersion in facts given from without, a new permission of intellectual adventure.[1] This apparent concession to the speculative metaphysician I welcomed, and was almost ready to call myself in that sense a convert to the pragmatic mode of expression. If I had been asked, I could not have named what seems to me a better example of the *intellectus sibi permissus* than Dr Schiller's *Riddles of the Sphinx*. In this attempt at approximation, however, I met with no encouragement. And in what is now written from the pragmatic point of view I feel more and more a steady drift to the overwhelming of all contemplation in the unexamined practical life of our day.

[1] See *The Metaphysics of Evolution*, pp. 395, 397–8, 439.

Among philosophers, I know as little where to look for a pure pragmatist as the pragmatists themselves profess to know where to look for "pure truth". From Prof. Muirhead's recent work dealing with Idealism in the English-speaking world,[1] I have learnt with pleasure that C. S. Peirce, the acute and stimulating American thinker (as he appears to me from report) who suggested the name, strongly repudiated the position of later pragmatism, that "we live for the sake of action", and held an unfavourable opinion on the "voluntarist" psychology of Wundt as applied to ethics. Now the psychology of Wundt and his disciples is claimed, on the whole rightly, as an aid by the pragmatists; though Wundt himself was not a pragmatist, but evidently thought that in his *System of Philosophy* he had arrived at something of the nature of "pure truth". In this complication, I have renounced the attempt to educe a pragmatic system from any of the actual representatives of the doctrine, and have tried to "construct" the pure pragmatist from the idea of

[1] *The Platonic Tradition in Anglo-Saxon Philosophy:* Studies in the History of Idealism in England and America. By John H. Muirhead (1931).

truth as "biological value". A systematic hunt for the type might perhaps resemble, on a smaller scale, that of Plato for "the sophist"; but I merely state the results.

If we go some way down the biological scale we shall find no difficulty. We need not even leave the vertebrata and turn to those favourites of the depreciators of conscious reason and extollers of instinctive "behaviour", the social insects. In a fine poem of Leconte de Lisle entitled *Sacra Fames*[1] the shark is represented as a kind of innocent monster— a monster only from our point of view—aiming simply at the preservation of organic life by his own mode of diet, and as completely clear of Hellenic addiction to the contemplative life as any pragmatist or dynamist or voluntarist or activist could desire.

> Certes, il n'a souci de l'immensité bleue,
> Des Trois Rois, du Triangle ou du long Scorpion
> Qui tord dans l'infini sa flamboyante queue,
> Ni de l'Ourse qui plonge au clair Septentrion.

A less purely innocent, a more sophisticated stage, is reached by the *Cyclops* of Euripides.[2] His way of

---

[1] *Poèmes Tragiques.*   [2] *Cycl.* 316 ff.

life also includes the eating of human flesh, but now with consciousness. He translates biological values into generalised economic laws. His "world-view" is sufficiently expressed in the first two lines of Shelley's translation:

Wealth, my good fellow, is the wise man's God,
All other things are a pretence and boast.

The wealth of the Cyclops was of course in flocks and herds; but no doubt the poet had in view the more abstractly conceived aims of still more sophisticated contemporaries. For our own time of "increasing purpose" in all the "Main Streets" of the world, the pragmatical wise man's position might be: Truth consists in the correlation of ideas useful to practical persons; the practical person being the person who can adapt himself with most efficiency to the modes of volitional activity, military or industrial or mixed, predominant in his own age.

The most recent development of the pragmatist theory of knowledge, in relation to its supposed scientific base, the voluntarist psychology, sometimes recalls to me Schopenhauer's fanciful idea that "epicycles of error", lasting about thirty years, present themselves from time to time as phases of fashionable philosophy under the illusion of "progress".[1] I shall not attempt a theory of the causes of this appearance, which would require more detailed psychological study than I have given to the subject, but shall turn to the positive side and try to show that sound theory of knowledge, spontaneously detaching itself from subordination to factors of volition directed to practice, has been evolved by the intellect as a continuous thread running through the history of philosophy. Theoretical tests of truth do not remain to be created, but already exist; and, with the aid of progressive scientific theory, can be applied to the investigation of the nature of reality.[2]

[1] Schopenhauer's metaphysical principle of "Will", I must note, does not make him a psychological voluntarist. In philosophical theory of knowledge he is a thoroughgoing intellectualist; as might be expected from his dictum that the superior man is two-thirds intellect and one-third will, the inferior man two-thirds will and one-third intellect.

[2] The voluntarist psychology is not necessarily incompatible with the belief in theoretic truth, though doubtless it gives a bias towards Pragmatism. I have myself recognised a certain advance made by it in opposing the apparent tendency of English Associationism to forget, in subjective analysis, the fundamentally teleological character of the

Quite consistently with this view, I am so far from denying the practical bearings of philosophic truth that, in my opinion, the whole future of humanity depends on direction by a true philosophy. But the possibility of attaining truth depends, I hold, on a certain disinterestedness. That is to say, philosophy must not take for postulates the purposes of those who govern or determine existing practice, but must make itself critical of practice in order to give it the right direction. The preparation for this direction, as Plato saw, is theoretical science in the widest sense. Now the type of mind from which this arises is one that, for voluntarist psychology as pragmatically applied, scarcely comes into view, perhaps even would be denied to exist.[1]

organism. (*The Metaphysics of Evolution*, p. 369.) Bain, however, who was both psychologist and philosopher, pointed out, in an article "On Association-Controversies" (*Mind*, April, 1887, pp. 181–2), that in an analytic account of the human mind the linking of mental elements according to laws of association must always have a far larger part than the classification of motives to acts of attention.

[1] See Dr Schiller's praise of Prof. McDougall (*Mind*, January, 1930, p. 110) for unreservedly proclaiming his adhesion to the pragmatic conception of science and truth, declaring that "all our intellectual apparatus and activities, the processes of perception, imagination, remembering, judgment, reasoning and so forth, are all alike, steps towards action, incidents, or events within a train of purposive activity

Plato, on the other hand, recognised in the theoretic impulse a factor that existed even in the minds of early men. The *Cratylus*, no doubt, is in part a satire on the etymologisers of the time; but between jest and earnest Socrates puts forward serious thoughts about the origin of language; and one of these appears to be that those who first gave names to things were no ordinary people (οὐ φαῦλοι), but were of the speculative tribe of subtle inquirers and reasoners; the kind of persons, in fact, who are sneered at by born pragmatists in all ages and nations as star-gazers and idle talkers.[1] This we may interpret as meaning that for them mental activity was not purely and simply an instrument for the preservation of organic life or for its quantitative

that tends to issue in action. We think, perceive, remember, judge or reason for the sake of action". Unless the word is used so as to include internal "action" of the mind, introspection directly refutes this. I do not, however, know the context of Prof. McDougall's statement.

[1] *Cratylus*, 401 B: κινδυνεύουσι γοῦν, ὠγαθὲ Ἑρμόγενες, οἱ πρῶτοι τὰ ὀνόματα τιθέμενοι οὐ φαῦλοι εἶναι ἀλλὰ μετεωρολόγοι καὶ ἀδολέσχαι τινές. For the sneering signification compare *Politicus*, 299 C. In the *Parmenides*, the aged philosopher advises the youthful Socrates to disregard this: ἕλκυσον δὲ σαυτὸν καὶ γύμνασον μᾶλλον διὰ τῆς δοκούσης ἀχρήστου εἶναι καὶ καλουμένης ὑπὸ τῶν πολλῶν ἀδολεσχίας, ἕως ἔτι νέος εἶ· εἰ δὲ μή, σὲ διαφεύξεται ἡ ἀλήθεια (135 D).

increase. Hobbes, two thousand years later, had the same thought when he described man as distinguished from other animals by the passions of admiration (*i.e.*, wonder) and curiosity; from which, he said, have sprung not only the invention of names but all science dependent on the investigation of causes (or, in the language of his time, philosophy).[1]

Even in cases where needs were assignable as the occasions on which sciences began, Aristotle (whom no one would class as an unpractical dreamer) ascribed their beginnings not to the practical need but to the opportunity of indulging theoretic curiosity. It was known that land-measurement was an end that the Egyptian geometers had to keep in view; but for Aristotle the fundamental reason explaining the rise of geometry in Egypt was not this, but the leisure enjoyed by the priestly caste. Whatever may be the truth here as regards the relation between external occasions and internal causes, we know that in Greece the passion for pure truth got

[1] *The Elements of Law, Natural and Politic*, ed. Tönnies, pp. 45–46. Cf. Plato, *Theaetetus*, 155 D, on wonder as the beginning of philosophy: μάλα γὰρ φιλοσόφου τοῦτο τὸ πάθος, τὸ θαυμάζειν· οὐ γὰρ ἄλλη ἀρχὴ φιλοσοφίας ἢ αὕτη.

loose, and that the Egyptian and Babylonian beginnings of geometry and astronomy were carried on
to the stage of theoretical science without further
reference to practice.

In the modern time also, as we can learn directly
from biography, scientific discoveries have not
usually been made by those in whom what are
commonly called practical motives are the most
powerful. Faraday deliberately left his electro-mag-
netic discoveries to be applied by others; and, even
in the case of invention directly for practice, the
result depends far more on intellectual facility in
combining ideas than on the quality of will in the
inventor, who is as a rule notoriously weak in
exploiting his inventions for his own advantage.
The union of intellectual and of active powers in the
same person has as much as anything the look of
accident.

But for the present topic, which is the determi-
nation of origins, the ancient history is the most
significant. As geometrical studies went on, there
seemed to arise in the human mind a new power
which cannot be described as volitional in any
distinctive sense, but only as intellectual. Early

methods of measurement such as may be compared
to a child's thought of cutting out and comparing
slips of paper, were superseded by reasoning from
the ideas of the figures constructed. With the
Pythagorean school there arose rational mathematics. And the truths attained survived not in
virtue of their useful applications, but through the
aptitude, in the small group of minds attracted to
the subject, for arriving at a common language
and so following in inter-communion the trains of
reasoning started by the initiators. This method,
however, did not solve the properly philosophical
problems that had already arisen on the borders of
the old Oriental and the new European civilisations.

The early Greek philosophers were at the same
time men of science, and, as Prof. Burnet has shown,
did not fail to practise the methods of observation
and experiment, though of course with no such
elaboration as modern instruments have made possible. Above all detailed research, such as their
Oriental predecessors had diligently pursued, there
was, however, a new aim. The distinctive effort of
the philosophers was, on the basis of their science,
and not by reconstruction of inherited religion, to

arrive at a view of the whole. Since the theories of individual thinkers, founded on partial aspects of the world, inevitably diverged, there arose as the second stage of philosophising the problem of the "test of truth". For mathematics this problem did not exist. The mathematicians, as Plato afterwards pointed out, proceeding on assumptions accepted as true within their own subject-matter, had demonstrations by which they could satisfy one another, and therefore did not need to turn back and examine first principles.

This does not mean that there was no contact between mathematical science and the thought that was concerned with the nature of things. The paradoxes of Zeno the Eleatic on motion were a prelude to the dialectic that became effective at Athens in the fifth century B.C. and culminated in the Aristotelian logic in the fourth. But this goes behind mathematics, and envelops it, with all other knowledge, in certain general requirements of correct reasoning. Its fundamental axiom, stated by Plato before Aristotle,[1] is the Law of Contradiction;

[1] Plato, *Rep.* IV, 436–438; Arist. *Met.* III, 6–8. Compare the "Eleatic Stranger" in the *Sophist*, 230 B, on the method used by those

which asserts that a thing cannot be and not be at the same time and in the same relation. Reduced to the utmost stringency by modern criticism, the law of contradiction is seen to be an axiom of valid thought, not a law of things; though we cannot reason correctly about things without presupposing it. If you have asserted a proposition with all due qualifications as to time and relation, you must not deny it in the same sense.[1] And, as Aristotle said, there is no mean: a proposition thus asserted is either true or false.[2] This is the Law of Excluded Middle; to which has been added the Law of Identity, which asserts that a thing is itself; not that it cannot change as time and relations change; but that, if you affirm a proposition about it in a certain

who set themselves to confute and expel erroneous beliefs: συνά-γοντες δὴ τοῖς λόγοις εἰς ταὐτὸν [τὰς δόξας] τιθέασι παρ' ἀλλήλας, τιθέντες δὲ ἐπιδεικνύουσιν αὐτὰς αὐταῖς ἅμα περὶ τῶν αὐτῶν πρὸς τὰ αὐτὰ κατὰ ταὐτὰ ἐναντίας.

If we are to accept it, on the authority of the "Epistles of Plato", that there was not and never was to be, a "philosophy of Plato", or at least that it is not to be found before the group beginning with the *Theaetetus*, why does the Eleatic Stranger talk in terms so very like those of Socrates in the *Republic*? (See Additional Note.)

[1] *Met.* III, 6, 1011 b 20: ἀδύνατον ἅμα καταφάναι καὶ ἀπο-φάναι ἀληθῶς.
[2] *Met.* III, 8, 1012 b 10: ἀνάγκη τῆς ἀντιφάσεως θάτερον εἶναι μόριον ἀληθές.

sense, you must in inferences from that proposition keep to that sense.

The method of disputation which implied those laws, when it was systematically used by Socrates to expose the incoherences of popular thinking, was much resented by the "practical men" of his time; and the formal logic founded on them by succeeding ages is now an object of extreme aversion to the pragmatists; who, however, would substitute, not the ancient method of rhetorical persuasion by unanalysed terms, but the still more rough and ready mode by which, in the order of nature, animal races are selected or eliminated. Is there not, they seem to say, the struggle for existence? Then let us throw out our hypotheses or our beliefs to sink or swim as the needs felt by the world determine.

The reply might be made, with a partial concession to their own point of view, that even the refinements of logic may have value in the struggle; but I take the ultimate reply to be that, whatever may be the fate of beliefs, "biological value" is the test only of survival, and that no jugglery with words can make "survival" signify "truth". Truth is not truth because it prevails;

though it may be true that it will prevail in the long run.

Against the notion of truth as pursued by Socrates, Plato and Aristotle, the pragmatists have shown signs of claiming as a precursor Protagoras, whose saying, "man is the measure of all things", in the "subjectivist" and "relativist" sense in which it is usually taken, seemed to tell in favour of their "scepticism of the instrument". This seems to mean that, since the human mind has been evolved under the condition that the human organism shall succeed in preserving itself under the stress of competition with other organisms, intelligence can have no value except in relation to that particular condition. It does not seem to have occurred to the "sceptics" that man, having won through the elementary struggle, may come to have other ends not expressible in terms of it. The famous maxim of Protagoras, under a benevolent (perhaps ultra-Platonic) interpretation, might easily pass into the declaration in Shelley's *Prometheus* that thought is the measure of the universe,—a postulate in some sense necessary to all philosophy. At any rate, the Platonic Protagoras cannot be claimed for the pecu-

16   IS THERE THEORETIC TRUTH?

liarly pragmatic fashion of scepticism; since, when
questioned by Socrates, he vehemently repudiates
the opinion of "the many", that knowledge is
simply the slave of need.[1] I am afraid that, if pragmatism wants a Platonic forerunner, it will have to
fall back on Dionysodorus, the less intelligent of the
two brothers in the *Euthydemus*. The old pancratiast,
turned amateur sophist, definitely proposes, as all-
sufficient, the criterion of being "up-to-date" and
ignoring anything said last year.[2]

If all that pragmatism meant was that the problems of practical life are among the occasions—and
among the most important occasions—of the search
for theoretical principles and methods, no one could
object. I have no doubt, for example, that the
discovery of the laws of thought had for its fairly
near source the law-courts and the public life of
Athens. The subtlest metaphysics of the ancient
world, as Vico said two centuries ago, had its
beginning in the habit of public debate in a demo-

[1] *Prot.* 352 B, C.
[2] *Euthyd.* 287 B : εἶτ', ἔφη, ὦ Σώκρατες, ὁ Διονυσόδωρος ὑπο-
λαβών, οὕτως εἶ Κρόνος, ὥστε ἃ τὸ πρῶτον εἴπομεν νῦν ἀνα-
μιμνήσκῃ, καὶ εἴ τι πέρυσιν εἶπον, νῦν ἀναμνησθήσῃ, τοῖς δ' ἐν
τῷ παρόντι λεγομένοις οὐχ ἕξεις ὅτι χρῇ ;

cracy.[1] We may see this reflected, and the dawn of the "laws of thought" appearing already, in the dramatic poets. In Aeschylus (*Eum.* 586) the rule of question and answer is stated: ἔπος δ' ἀμείβου πρὸς ἔπος ἐν μέρει τιθείς. In Euripides (*Alc.* 528), Heracles, whom we may very well take as representing "the plain man", denies the compatibility of to be and not to be: χωρὶς τό τ' εἶναι καὶ τὸ μὴ νομίζεται. Thus, through the life of legal and political discussion, a language was formed that could be made the instrument of inquiry into the mind itself as well as into things. It is more to the Athenian democracy than to mathematical science that we owe the series, Socrates, Plato, Aristotle, as we know it historically. Hence the profound pathos of the *Crito* when Socrates imagines the laws of Athens as telling him that all his life he has acquiesced in them, and must therefore submit to the sentence pronounced on him unjustly, though not by them yet by the Athenians.

On the relation between the work of Socrates and of Plato, I have seen no good reason for changing the view that has usually been inferred from the

[1] See the third of my series of articles on Vico, *Mind*, July, 1926, p. 325.

statements of Aristotle; namely (to put it in terms
not yet extant, though they arose on the line of
Platonic thought) that Socrates threw his strength
into educing the concept or the "universal" from
the particulars of experience,[1] and that Plato went
on to a theory of the realities corresponding to the
mental concept, and gave the name of Idea to the
Reality. What we have to avoid is the attempt to
make the divisions too rigorous, as Aristotle, working with definitions framed by himself, may have
done. To sum up Plato's whole thought in formulae
taken from the *Metaphysics* ought of course to be
regarded as necessarily inadequate to a developing
theory; but the formulae cannot be ignored as a
guide to understanding; and I do not see how it can
be maintained that Aristotle was "too late" to
count as a judge of any difference there may have
been between "the historical" and "the Platonic"
Socrates.

The essential correction to be made in any historical schematism whatever, comes from recognising

---

[1] Plato himself has made Socrates mark off the nature of man
as having the power to form concepts. See *Phaedrus*, 249 B: δεῖ
γὰρ ἄνθρωπον συνιέναι κατ᾽ εἶδος λεγόμενον, ἐκ πολλῶν ἰὸν
αἰσθήσεων εἰς ἓν λογισμῷ συναιρούμενον.

that the transitions from one way of thinking to another could not have been actually so abrupt as they are made to appear in a compressed statement. For example, I fully concede to recent criticism that it would be unintelligible that Socrates, living when he did, should never at any time of his life have felt any interest in physical questions, but should have turned at once from the naturalistic inquiries by which he was surrounded in his youth to an exclusive occupation with human conduct. And it would be astonishing if Plato, perpetually occupied as he evidently was in critical return on thoughts he had dramatically put forth, should not have been more distinctively Socratic in his earlier than in his later Dialogues—even if, as I hold, continuity was never lost. This being allowed, there is no difficulty in supposing that the word "Idea" (ἰδέα or εἶδος) passed on from the master to the disciple not without enlargement in signification, but without the violence of change that would have made the name of Socrates inappropriate to the thoughts expressed.

To suppose "Idea" to have been simply a technical term, of Pythagorean origin, meaning "Form", is quite incompatible with the constant reference in the Dialogues to the internal activity of the mind in the quest of it; and we have independent evidence for this "subjective" significance. When Aristophanes claims credit for his unceasing preoccupation with the introduction of "new ideas" (καινὰς ἰδέας, *Nubes*, 547), the literal translation is the best available. Whether a modern dramatic author, if he said a similar thing, would be looking more into his own thought, while Aristophanes, being as an ancient presumably more "objective", had his mind more fixed on an imaginary stage, it seems to me impossible to say. What is clear is that the word was not purely technical and quasi-geometrical, but in colloquial usage carried with it a mental reference not invented in the schools.

In what appears to be Plato's maturest thought, the Idea is declared not to be purely and simply something in the mind, but also not to be without mind or life. Of course it is not an image: Coleridge's antithesis between "clear ideas" and "distinct images" indicates excellently its peculiar relation to the concept. Yet even the notion of an image is used by Plato in a fundamental passage[1]

[1] *Phaedo*, 99 D–100 A.

to make the effort to attain truth by Ideas intelligible.

This is the famous passage about the second voyage in search of the Cause (δεύτερος πλοῦς ἐπὶ τὴν τῆς αἰτίας ζήτησιν). I have met with the comment that by the δεύτερος πλοῦς is not to be understood a "second best", a makeshift where we are at a loss, but a more difficult and abstruse way of seeking the causes of things than the obvious direct one.[1] I do not remember whether the remark has also been made that it is in fact equivalent to Kant's "Copernican change of standpoint"; but it evidently is the first expression on record of that mental revolution—not made once for all but repeated at intervals by thinkers before Kant, and ever in need of renewal. Thought about things, and not the naked vision of the external thing itself, is to be recognised as the way to learn what is real and what is not. The mind, as Socrates puts it, becomes dazzled by the attempt to investigate things directly, as the eye becomes dazzled by gazing on an eclipse of the sun instead of viewing its reflexion as an

[1] It does, however, mean a "second best" in *Politicus*, 300 C, and in *Philebus*, 19 C.

image. As we aid the sight by substituting the image for the sun itself, so let us turn to the investigation of things by the forms of discourse in which they are expressed. And yet perhaps this comparison is not altogether exact. It is only by way of illustration that we have spoken of "images"; for it is not by any means to be conceded that when we are dealing with things in discourse of reason we are dealing more with images of them and less with true reality than when we see them in action.[1] The method of search, Socrates proceeds, is to aim at a consistency attainable only by reasoning so as to eliminate contradictions in reference to the realities expressed by general terms—in short, the Ideas.

Nothing could more clearly indicate the affinity of the realities called Ideas to mind and not to some object apparently grasped in a vision of the external. Plato's idealism is not precisely that of any modern thinker, nor even of Neo-Platonism; but the later

[1] *Phaedo*, 99 E–100 A: ἔδοξε δή μοι χρῆναι εἰς τοὺς λόγους καταφυγόντα ἐν ἐκείνοις σκοπεῖν τῶν ὄντων τὴν ἀλήθειαν. ἴσως μὲν οὖν ᾧ εἰκάζω τρόπον τινὰ οὐκ ἔοικεν· οὐ γὰρ πάνυ συγχωρῶ τὸν ἐν λόγοις σκοπούμενον τὰ ὄντα ἐν εἰκόσι μᾶλλον σκοπεῖν ἢ τὸν ἐν ἔργοις. Cf. *Leges*, X, 897 D, E.

doctrines are more or less derivative species of the same genus.

The procedure set forth is evidently, in psychological terms, by way of concepts; but it has been observed that in the *Phaedo* there are germs of the empirical psychology of Association, applied since to the theory of percepts and images. Of this there is also a sketch in one of Aristotle's minor psychological tracts, the *De Memoria et Reminiscentia*; and Aristotle in the *De Anima*, with more detachment than his master from general philosophical and ethical points of view, founded the positive science of psychology on a broad basis, proceeding upwards from biology, of which he was also one of the founders. Partly influenced by Aristotle, there arose the powerful "naturalistic" systems of Epicureanism and Stoicism, appealing in principle to perception and experimental tests; but these tests in antiquity remained relatively undeveloped. The most definitive result of the great period of Greek philosophy was the logic of Aristotle, proceeding from conception and the laws of thought. When Aristotle had done his work, it could be said that, through the investigation of the concept, resolutely taken in hand by Socrates, and carried forward to new issues by Plato, the Hellenic mind had passed on to a phase in which canons of thinking were established that were irrefragable within their limits. This is not to say that the ancients had completed even the theory of logic; but they had laid one permanent foundation for all future time.

Meanwhile mathematics and mathematical astronomy continued to be cultivated as pure science, especially in the Academic school founded by Plato, of which Euclid of Alexandria is known to have been an adherent. The Alexandrian mathematicians, by working out the geometrical theory of conic sections, prepared an instrument for the development that began nearly two thousand years later, when Kepler on a basis of observation, with the aid thus furnished in advance by the ancient geometry, proved that the planets move not in circles or combinations of circles but in ellipses. This used to be a stock illustration of the unforeseen value of the pursuit of pure truth; but perhaps the pragmatists will tell us that the Alexandrian geometry was not "true" till the development of Copernicanism by means of it had been proved to be applicable to navigation.[1] Even when the experimental sciences are in question, they do not seem to distinguish very accurately between application and verification. A pupil of Euclid, indeed, is said not to have been satisfied with the "biological value" of the exercise involved in drawing diagrams, but to have asked what he was to get by all that trouble; whereupon the geometer commissioned a slave to give the young pragmatist a coin, since he must make something out of his learning.

But we must return to the question of philosophic truth. Plato, notwithstanding his high regard for mathematical science, insisted that it is not philosophy; which does not consist in following a train of deductive reasoning from point to point without turning back on the premises, but in the "dialectical" giving and receiving of reasons. For this, mathematicians are seldom competent.[2] This was no doubt true in principle; but, on the one side, Plato's dialectical criticisms of popular modes of persuasion did not effectively modify the predominance of

[1] Whether the substitution of the Copernican for the Ptolemaic astronomy necessarily makes a difference to navigation I do not know.
[2] *Rep.* VII, 531 D, E. Cf., on the "test of truth", *Leges*, XII, 966 B.

rhetoric in ancient education; and, on the other side, too much insistence on theory of knowledge (called by Aristotle "first philosophy") and on logical method began after a time to have a sterilising influence on science. In the Middle Ages, with their religion of authority founded on tradition, so many essentially empirical assertions were taken for granted without reference to the appropriate test of experience—insufficiently elaborated in the Aristotelian logic, far as Aristotle himself was from ignoring experience—that all the care taken over correctness of reasoning seemed to lead only to empty logomachy. Thus, after a period of widespread revolt from Aristotle, who, having been enthroned as the supreme authority in human knowledge, was unjustly blamed for the spirit of verbal dogmatism that had taken possession of the mediaeval schools, two new departures began, one on the Continent and one in England.[1]

With Descartes there came a turning away from the formal logic or dialectic of the schools (though he could not escape its influence) to mathematical

[1] This is a very broad statement, and requires much qualification in detail.

science as the model. Himself a mathematician of genius, he was attracted precisely by the apparently straightforward course of mathematical deduction to incontestable truth; and so conceived the idea of applying mathematical method everywhere. England, as well as France, was to produce mathematicians of genius; but its most characteristic philosophical minds were without the special bent to mathematics. Thus the divergence from ancient ways was more radical, and for a time opposition to Descartes was combined with opposition to the Scholasticism still taught officially in all the Universities of Europe. The English philosophers looked away from the academic teaching to the reviving sciences of observation and experiment; and in theory of knowledge Locke, after the diverse preludes of Bacon and Hobbes, struck out the distinctively English line. The English idea, now become revolutionary, was, broadly, verification by perception as the way of establishing general truths. In pure theory of knowledge Locke, on one side the opponent, was on the other side the continuator of Descartes. Like Descartes, he sought primary certitude in examination of the contents of the mind itself;

thus taking over, in his turn, the legacy which the ancient schools had bequeathed to the Middle Ages; but, while the more directly Platonising Descartes found certainty in what he called "innate ideas" (general notions which the adult mind discovers by looking into itself), Locke insisted above all on investigation of what the Platonists called "genesis". By the "plain historical way" we must set ourselves to learn first how the mind grows. Only thus may we hope to discover what it is capable of knowing.

The Experientialism of Locke and his successors, it may be summarily stated, over a large part of the field of knowledge, has conquered Europe; but again, for the progress that comes by degrees from action and reaction, a recoil was necessary. The history of the recoil in England, starting from that study of German thought which began effectively both in England and in France with the nineteenth century, is particularly instructive.

Near the middle of the century, J. S. Mill's *System of Logic, Ratiocinative and Inductive*, was hailed as the final triumph of the experiential philosophy. With some qualifications, it has since been incorporated in the official teaching of Logic. Even the representatives of surviving Scholasticism, little as they might like Mill's aims, could not deny the need of a supplement to the meagre "logic of induction" hitherto current in the schools, and they recognised that Mill had done at last effectively what Bacon in the *Novum Organum* had only projected. Mill, however, left some important points of principle indeterminate; and Herbert Spencer, who was classed with him as the other great protagonist of science and experience, was too much occupied in systematising knowledge under the new formula of Evolution to deal very exactly with the underlying metaphysical questions. Now for a long time Kant and Hegel had been great names with the opponents of the English philosophical tradition; and at length a dominant leader arose in T. H. Green, who successfully urged the philosophic youth of Britain —or the larger part of it—to wake up from insular slumber and enter upon the neglected heritage of a thought deeper and higher than that of the unspiritual eighteenth century. Beyond that limited "Enlightenment", English philosophy had failed to advance; Mill and Spencer being, though later, less profound and penetrating than Hume in the *Treatise of Human Nature*; a work that had been forgotten even by Hume's readers, who accepted his own judgment in preferring the easier *Inquiry*. Green accordingly, in the celebrated Introductions to his edition of Hume, put all his power into showing that on the ground of Experientialism, as laid bare by Hume's sceptical thought, there can be no constructive philosophy.

The content of the new doctrine, on the positive side, is out of the range of the present discussion,[1] which concerns the form rather than the matter of knowledge; but I may now express the opinion that the result was in the long run a gain as preventing the reign of a new dogmatism. I lay special stress on a point of scientific interest which the school, preoccupied as it was with the ethical and religious aspects of philosophy, perhaps did not duly enforce. In spite of its attachment to Kant (who with

[1] An account, both sympathetic and critical, of the contributions made to philosophy by the representatives of the school is given in *Neo-Hegelianism*, by Prof. Hiralal Haldar (1927). This has recently been supplemented by Prof. J. H. Muirhead's work mentioned above (p. 3), which deals circumstantially with the preparation for the movement in earlier English philosophy and with its larger aspects as a mode of Platonising Idealism.

some of the school had more influence than Hegel),
I do not remember that Kant's unique importance
in the theory of mathematical knowledge was ever
adequately dwelt on. Yet this was precisely the
point where the traditional "English philosophy"
had failed to keep up with a real advance of thought.
For I do not agree with those who, while admiring
Kant's immense architectonic power, regard him as
unable to arrive at the solution of any specific problem. I hold that he did actually solve the question,
never let go by the ancient successors of Plato, why
mathematics is entitled to a peculiar position between formal logic and the sciences of experience.
The reason is that it arises from the power of the
intellect, through the very nature of space and number, to arrive within their range at "synthetic
judgments *a priori*"; that is, necessary truths not
derived by the laws of thought from the mere
implications of preceding assertions, but constructed
by a mental activity going forth without waiting for
impressions received. Natural science indeed arrives
at "synthetic judgments"; that is, judgments not
purely "analytic" as resulting from mere formal
inference; but in natural science experience has to be

waited for or sought out before inferences can be drawn. In mathematics the mind itself constructs the truths which it necessarily affirms.

Kant's own prediction that his philosophy would be understood in the twentieth century is receiving some confirmation from the eminent mathematicians of the present time. Sir James Jeans seems to be even ultra-Kantian when he says, distinguishing between pure and mixed mathematics: "By 'pure mathematics' is meant those departments of mathematics which are creations of pure thought, of reason operating solely within her own sphere, as contrasted with 'applied mathematics' which reasons about the external world, after first taking some supposed property of the external world as its raw material".[1]

Acceptance of this general view need not mean that either mathematicians or psychologists can have no new subtleties to propound on Kant's language, or that the last word has been said. What I mean is that Kant seized his own problem as Aristotle and Mill seized theirs, and in effect solved it. It may indeed seem paradoxical that Kant, who is said to

[1] *The Mysterious Universe*, p. 130.

have had only an ordinary knowledge of mathematics, solved a problem concerning their own
science that had escaped philosophers of mathematical genius like Descartes and Leibniz. There is no
more difficulty in allowing this, however, than in
allowing that Mill, who knew the methods and
details of experimental science more from books
eagerly read than from the laboratory, solved the
problem of inductive logic. To apprehend a question of philosophical principle is not necessarily the
result of skill in the special branch of science dealt
with. Comte, for example, who was a mathematician of some originality, made acute observations
on mathematical science; but within the science and
without examining its foundations. For example, I
cannot help thinking that he improves on Newton
when he substitutes, for the description of algebra
as a generalised or universalised arithmetic, the
distinction between arithmetic and algebra as
the "calculus of values" and the "calculus of functions"; the infinitesimal calculus being further distinguished as calculus of "indirect functions". On
the other hand, Comte was even more remote than
Mill from any attempt to solve Kant's problem. In

general philosophy he belongs entirely to the experiential succession (called English), which on the
Continent had gone further along the path of
empiricism than Locke; and he simply takes for
granted that mathematics can be treated as a natural
science of experiences received. Yet his mathematical training had an important influence on his
philosophy. The application of mathematics to
natural phenomena gave him, as Renouvier (another eminent philosopher trained in mathematical
physics) has pointed out, the idea of physical *law*;
and Comte's formulations of this in the successive
volumes of the *Philosophie Positive* told powerfully
on the development of Mill's *Logic*. Mill himself was
well instructed in mathematics, had been trained
both in the logic of Aristotle and in its scholastic
derivative, and claimed a share in the inheritance of
the Platonic dialectic. With this preparation, he was
able to fix the problem set by induction as a way of
discovering truth, and to see that it was not yet
solved.

Mill solved the problem of inductive logic by
showing how from particular experiences general
laws can be arrived at by means of deduction from

a principle called the Uniformity of Nature. Given this principle, "that what happens once, will, under a sufficient degree of similarity of circumstances, happen again, and not only again, but as often as the same circumstances recur",[1] certain "canons of induction" can be constructed by which determinate sequences of phenomena called "laws of nature" may be established. Now the Uniformity of Nature is not a mathematical axiom, but is the ground for the application of mathematics to nature. Obviously, if we could not trust to the repetition of like phenomena under like circumstances, our mental constructions in space and number could never furnish us with the means to "indirect measurement" of quantities in the world of phenomena. Comte therefore welcomed the *Logic*; though he regarded Mill as not quite clear of the "metaphysical" stage. If he had attained complete "positivity", the purely phenomenal character of science would have been clear to him without the need of probing its foundations.

Thinkers more metaphysical than Mill objected that the probing had not gone far enough. The

[1] *Logic*, Book III, chap. iii, § 1.

unsatisfactory part of Mill's doctrine as theory of knowledge was that, through fear of "the *a priori*", he tried to derive the principle of all natural science from that which is admitted to be the weakest form of induction; namely, "induction by simple enumeration", a mere summation of particular experiences. Against this, and against the associationist psychology which with Mill sometimes did duty for the metaphysical analysis by which it ought to have been continued, F. H. Bradley, the most subtle psychologist and dialectician of the school opposed to the traditional English Experientialism, drove home the argument that from mere particulars, without universals, no step can be taken in valid reasoning from experience. This, however, does not mean that the experiential logic of Mill was overthrown, but only that his philosophical theory of knowledge, his "first philosophy" in Aristotle's sense, needed revision. And, on Bradley's side, there was an approximation later to English psychological methods. He is known to have ranked very high the treatise of W. Volkmann, which differs from English psychological work less in method than in its more systematic carrying through of

Herbartian developments associationist in principle.[1] And the Absolute of Bradley was in the end a kind of Experience.

We are reminded here of the importance of psychology, or of the psychological attitude, at the chief turning-points, both ancient and modern, in the history of philosophy. With this view, English thought in particular has been so imbued that psychology has tended to be confused with philosophy in the proper sense of the term. Psychology itself, or the scientific study of mind, inevitably turns back critically on what we think we know of external things; and so the science of human nature, or of the human understanding, has sometimes been regarded as doing duty for the whole of reflective knowledge; and philosophy, which is incomplete without Ontology—the doctrine of Being—has suffered. On the other hand, as Croom Robertson said in developing this view,[2] Kant, because he was (in spite of his "Copernican change of standpoint") less

[1] At the suggestion of Croom Robertson, I wrote an exposition of Volkmann's *Lehrbuch der Psychologie* which appeared in *Mind*, July and October, 1890.

[2] See the article "Psychology and Philosophy" in *Philosophical Remains*.

explicitly pyschological, made the truth in his philosophy less generally accessible.

What has been gained, or ought to have been
gained, in the passage from ancient to modern
Idealism, is, indeed, the greater accessibility that
comes from closer examination of the empirical
components of knowledge, as distinguished from
ever greater refinement in analysis of concepts. In
spite of many difficulties in the work, I cannot find
a better expression of the ultimate modern point of
view than in Prof. Whitehead's great effort in constructive philosophy, called by him "the philosophy
of organism".[1] "The subjectivist principle is that the
whole universe consists of elements disclosed in the
analysis of the experiences of subjects. Process is the
becoming of experience. It follows that the philosophy of organism entirely accepts the subjectivist
bias of modern philosophy. It also accepts Hume's
doctrine that nothing is to be received into the
philosophical scheme which is not discoverable as an
element in subjective experience. This is the ontological principle." We have here, however, only one

[1] *Process and Reality:* An Essay in Cosmology (1929). See Part II,
chap. vii, § 5, p. 233.

side of Prof. Whitehead's doctrine. Following what
is in itself a hopeful method, he turns back to the
earlier philosophies of Descartes and Locke, who for
modern times were the sources of the "subjectivist
bias", and tries to find in the "surd" of their
systems, the dualism and realism banished by
Spinoza on the one side and by Berkeley and Hume
on the other, elements of neglected truth. I am
obliged to confess that for me this brings back the
"dazzling" described in the *Phaedo* as the result of
the strain after direct vision of entities in the external
world; and that, though the later thinkers also are
of course not final, I have been apt to regard them
as offering a purified version of the philosophical
truths brought to light by Descartes and Locke.
From this starting-point, I shall try to re-state, with
the most denuded simplicity, what seems to me the
clear result of modern idealism as regards the external world.

To avoid being taken for a solipsist, I must pre-
mise that when Prof. Whitehead puts the alternative:[1] "Science is *either* an important statement
of systematic theory correlating observations of a

[1] *Process and Reality*, Part IV, chap. v, § 4, p. 468.

common world, *or* is the daydream of a solitary intelligence with a taste for the daydream of publication", I completely accept the former position.
This I do not find to be at all inconsistent with the
statement that the perceptions which seem to give
the most direct knowledge of the things around us
can all be resolved into mental processes without
any residue enabling us to say anything about a
"pure" object independent of perception. As
Berkeley showed: if you take away from the account of body or matter everything that can be
psychologically expressed, nothing expressible remains. We are left with the result that whatever we
can know as existent is potentially capable of an
expression in consciousness: otherwise we could
not know it. It is of no avail to try to separate off
the correlates of the senses of touch and pressure
as primary qualities—qualities really in things—
against the secondary qualities correlated with
sound, colour, taste and smell, which exist only "in
us". These are as much parts of experience as the
former, and all we know in all cases is the "idea"
(which for Locke and Berkeley included percepts
as well as images), with the coexistences and se-

quences among ideas. Berkeley himself, for an
ontological account, went on to suppose "ideas"
as something permanent in the mind of God; but
this, in the later developments of Berkeleyanism,
easily came to be regarded as theological presupposition, not as logical consequence. The Berkeleyan
idealist finds himself left, not with an immediate
solution, but with a not yet solved problem of
ontology. It is quite clear to him, however, that no
ontology can be directly given by physics. Hume's
examination of causality reinforced this conclusion
by showing with more circumstance that no sequence in the external world can be inferred *a priori*:
for our inferences of what will happen in the future,
we depend on experiences of what has happened
in the past, and we cannot discover any intrinsic
reason for the actual succession of events.[1]

The modern "mechanical philosophy" indeed,
with certain concessions of its own which quite
separated it from "naïve realism", had a very plausible case for its claim to represent pure truth of

[1] For the close relation here between the two thinkers, compare
with Hume's demonstrations the anticipatory expressions in Berkeley's
Principles of Human Knowledge, § 31.

science. Some appearances were taken to be more expressive of reality than others because they point to a persistence—as, for example, of weight—that continues through the flux of all the rest. The "corpuscles" of the moderns, like the atoms of Democritus and Epicurus, could be supposed the enduring basis of the resistance opposed by the object to efforts on our part to move it. By hypothesis they were correlates of the senses of touch and pressure. Thus they were conformable to the preference given to those senses as tokens of reality. By the Berkeleyan subjective method, however, the very acute argumentation of Lucretius against the partisans of another sense—that of heat—could be retorted on his own position. Against the atom of Epicurus, the Stoics took as the ground of physical explanation the Heraclitean "fire", imagined by them as the primeval element from which all the other elements emerge and into which they are resolved. But out of fire, the Epicurean poet insists,[1] nothing can be made but modifications in the quality of heat. All the various qualities of things known by the other senses—the senses, in terms of

[1] *De Rerum Natura*, I, 635–704.

modern psychology, other than the sense of temperature—remain unexplained.

> Nam cur tam variae res possent esse requiro,
> Ex uno si sunt igni puroque creatae.

The Stoic theorist tries to set sense against sense,
whereas all the senses alike have their claims to
determine belief in their objects.

> Nam contra sensus ab sensibus ipse repugnat
> Et labefactat eos, unde omnia credita pendent,
> Unde hic cognitus est ipsi quem nominat ignem.
> Credit enim sensus ignem cognoscere vere,
> Cetera non credit, quae nilo clara minus sunt.

But clearly, it might have been argued against the
atomist, out of tangibility you can get nothing but
tangibility, as the Heraclitean can get nothing out of
data of the sense that reveals heat but more or less
heated aggregates. And in fact all the topics of scepticism were brought into play in antiquity against the
notion that objects can be immediately grasped (or
"prehended") as entities. To the continued polemic
of the New Academics and the Pyrrhonists, Stoicism
and Epicureanism intellectually succumbed; leaving
the ground clear for the constructive idealism of
the Neo-Platonists. When the sciences revived,

after the long succeeding period of neglect or slow and episodic progress, new forms of the old philosophical controversies naturally returned with them.

To produce popular effect, what the modern idealistic criticism needed was some confirmation from a process within physical science itself. This has not come till our own time, but it has come with surprising effectiveness; surprising because the new physics is even more abstruse than those types of difficulty, the philosophies of Kant and Hegel. Hitherto, though Berkeley had proved in his *Theory of Vision* that our apparent direct knowledge of extension and extended things is really the result of experiences of conjunctions between tactile and visual "ideas"; though Hume had proved that prior to experience we have no knowledge as to what will be the behaviour of visible and tangible objects when brought into relation with one another; and though Kant had found space not to be something directly known to us as an external vacuity, but to be a "form" in which the mind places phenomena; yet the prestige of the "mechanical philosophy" as a doctrine concerning reality may be said to have grown continually from the seventeenth to the latter part of the nineteenth century. Philosophical men of science might see that the conclusions of Berkeley, Hume and Kant, at least in their negative or sceptical aspect, were irrefutable; but the mechanical (or, as perhaps it might be more accurately called, the kinetic[1]) view of nature remained a system that seemed not only thinkable but imaginable. Besides, actual science was always making progress in virtue of the presupposition that the phenomena of nature admit of explanation from hidden groupings of particles visible and tangible for finer senses (if we had them) and now concentrated and now dispersed in otherwise empty space. The newer science, however, making no philosophical assumptions, and proceeding by mathematical reasoning not fully intelligible to any but experts, has found that the "classical mechanics", while it is "nearly right" for the mass of verifiable results,

[1] Dr Merz suggests this alternative name in his *History of European Thought in the Nineteenth Century*, vol. II, chap. vi.

Modern science, we must remember, is so abstract that it speaks of mechanism without μηχανή, dynamics without δύναμις, and psychology without ψυχή. But Lucretius had already eliminated the notion of contrivance from "mechanism" when he spoke of the "moles et machina mundi" (v, 96).

fails to conform, when strictly examined, to the last refinements of astronomical observation. Also, in physics and chemistry, the "hard atom", which had done duty through all changes of theory from Leucippus and Democritus onward, has had to give place to something, namely, the electron, which is no longer an object of imaginative sense, but only a symbol. For the electron is not to be conceived as a correlate of the senses that gave most conviction of certainty—namely, sight and touch—and is definable by no sense at all that we possess in distinction from other senses. So far as the universal medium, the "ether" of the physicists, is concerned, half the scientific world has yielded to criticisms anticipated by Comte and Mill from their experientialist and phenomenist point of view. The phenomena of light present many resemblances to the phenomena of vibrating bodies; but we are not justified in saying that they are actually the results of vibration.

The most eminent men of science at the present time are the most resolute in stating such conclusions. The final positions of Sir James Jeans and Sir Arthur Eddington scarcely fall short of Berkeleyan idealism; as may be shown by two quotations.

If we must have a model of the physical world, says Jeans,[1] the electron and proton must be represented by the simplest things known to us, tiny hard spheres. "The model works well for a time and then suddenly breaks in our hands....A hard sphere has always a definite position in space; the electron apparently has not. A hard sphere takes up a very definite amount of room,—an electron—well,... perhaps the best answer is that it takes up the whole of space."[2]

Now compare Eddington:[3] "If actuality means 'known to mind', then it is a purely subjective character of the world; to make it objective we must substitute 'knowable to mind'. The less stress we lay on the accident of parts of the world being known at the present era to particular minds, the more stress we must lay on the *potentiality* of being known to mind as a fundamental objective property of matter, giving it a status of actuality whether

[1] *The Universe Around Us*, pp. 133–4.
[2] I had suggested (*The Metaphysics of Evolution*, p. 437) that its reality is not in space—which amounts to the same thing. The reality being properly at no point, and the manifestation virtually everywhere, there can be transference of appearance from point to point without interval of time.
[3] *The Nature of the Physical World*, p. 267.

individual consciousness is taking note of it or not".

Are we then, for safety, to fall back on the phenomenism of Comte and Mill, not trying to find in scientific hypotheses more than devices for predicting appearances according to laws of coexistence and succession, or shall we, going beyond Hume and Kant, put forth on the sea of ontology? I propose that we should attempt the voyage, on the basis suggested by those men of science who are not only ready themselves to follow the idealistic argument, whether modern or ancient, but are busily engaged in conjectures of their own that can only be called philosophical.

So far as the past is concerned, we have seen, much is secure. We have intellectual principles of formal logic, of mathematics, and at least of phenomenal science. But a previous question remains: Are we entitled to go further?

II

HAS ONTOLOGY FAILED?

As a precedent, we may appeal to what Socrates says in the *Meno*, that we shall be better in every way for not assuming that that which no one knows cannot be found out.[1] The unknown is not necessarily unknowable.

Yes, it may be said, that is all very well in the detailed investigations of science; but has it not been proved that the ultimately real being of the universe must baffle all inquiry? And, it may be urged against those who still find encouragement in Plato for aiming at an ontology: was not negation the final result of the sustained effort of Plato's own school? The New Academy provided the best-furnished arsenal of weapons of scepticism in antiquity; and, after Platonism had again become constructive, one of the last survivors of Neo-Platonism,

[1] Plato, *Meno*, 86 B: ὅτι δ' οἰόμενοι δεῖν ζητεῖν ἃ μή τις οἶδεν βελτίους ἂν εἶμεν καὶ ἀνδρικώτεροι καὶ ἧττον ἀργοὶ ἢ εἰ οἰοίμεθα ἃ μὴ ἐπιστάμεθα μηδὲ δυνατὸν εἶναι εὑρεῖν μηδὲ δεῖν ζητεῖν, περὶ τούτου πάνυ ἂν διαμαχοίμην, εἰ οἷός τε εἴην, καὶ λόγῳ καὶ ἔργῳ.

Damascius, laid so much stress on the agnostic element in the Neo-Platonic ontology or theology that he ended by literally anticipating Herbert Spencer; sending forth a book *On First Principles* (περὶ τῶν πρώτων ἀρχῶν) in which he outwent all his predecessors in the strength of his declarations that the principle called in the school the One is completely unknowable. Moreover, the beginning of this development can be traced back to Plato himself, whose two unknowables, we may put it, became for his successors one unknowable. In the *Republic*, Socrates makes the Idea of the Good the principle of the world of reality, but is so far from professing to know what it is that he places it "beyond Being". And, in the *Parmenides*, the chief of the Eleatic school, with which Plato undoubtedly claimed kinship, is made to show that his own principle called there the One can equally well have all predicates applied to it and be deprived of all predicates. The principle, then, under this name also is placed at its summit "beyond Being". The "One without predicates" was recognised by Plotinus as pre-eminently "the One"; as a new "hypothesis" of the Platonic Parmenides, not to be found in the

HAS ONTOLOGY FAILED? 51

poem of Parmenides himself; and as identical with
the Idea of the Good in the *Republic*.[1] In the tradition
of the ages it became the source of that "negative
theology" which was held to be the profoundest.
Hamilton and Mansel were still within the range of
the thought; and both Spencer and Huxley have
acknowledged their influence. Agnosticism thus did
not spring up merely from a modern vision of the increase of nescience that ever accompanies the increase
of science, but has a long pedigree both philosophical
and theological. Can we hope to go deeper?

I reply that the agnostic aspect of the great constructive thinkers of the past must not be construed
too strictly. The paradox is merely in form when
Spencer says that the Unknowable is the Cause of the

[1] Prof. E. R. Dodds, in an article on "The *Parmenides* of Plato and
the Neo-Platonic 'One'" (*The Classical Quarterly*, July–October,
1928), has quite rightly pointed out that in *The Neo-Platonists* I did not
sufficiently stress the Neo-Platonic identification of the Idea of the
Good in the *Republic* with the One of the *Parmenides*. There is, indeed, as
he notes, a passing reference (2nd ed. p. 56); but this is only to the recognition by Plotinus (*Enn.* v, i, 8) that the distinctions drawn by the
Platonic Parmenides go (as Proclus afterwards showed more elabo-
rately) beyond anything to be found in the historical Parmenides: ὁ δὲ
παρὰ Πλάτωνι Παρμενίδης ἀκριβέστερον λέγων διαιρεῖ ἀπ' ἀλλή-
λων τὸ πρῶτον ἕν, ὃ κυριώτερον ἕν, καὶ δεύτερον ἓν πολλὰ λέγων,
καὶ τρίτον ἕν καὶ πολλά. Prof. Dodds tries to determine how and when
the identification, which he places before Plotinus, had been made.

4-2

Knowable, or when Bradley treats Appearance as the manifestation of Reality or the Absolute. It is possible that in philosophy, as sometimes in art, the way of advance may be to go back provisionally to the formative stages of past thought or vision, rather than to the stages of relative fixation. Thus the growing point of present effort to something new may be reinforced. And the vital and positive effort of ancient philosophy lasted a long time.

From Plato's Good beyond Being an attempt has been made to develop the very modern speculation that a non-existent ideal is the end to which the activity of the human race may make nearer and nearer approaches, but which is never attained. This has usually been rejected as evidently, however plausible to a mind familiar with modern evolutionary theories, not Plato's meaning; and I agree with the rejection. Indeed Vacherot, who wrote the most stimulating of the brilliant French books dealing with Neo-Platonism, and himself held a view about the relation between the real and the ideal something like this, developed his doctrine not out of Plato or Plotinus, but rather in opposition to what he conceived to be their ultimate philosophy; which places the highest thin s first in order. Yet, while the explanation offered was wrong, I think it pointed to at least part of the meaning in referring the Idea of the Good to a teleological process; and I would translate it into modern terms in some such way as the following.

The Ideas may be described as certain perdurable conditions which make possible the existence of the "kinds" corresponding to scientifically attained concepts. These conditions are to be regarded as more real than their manifestations in the world of flux. Now a part of the activity in the world as it appears consists in the pursuit of what are thought to be "goods" by the individuals in it. We cannot describe any one "kind" of thing as the one good for all; but we can say with certainty that pursuit of ends regarded as goods goes on in our world. Teleology, in short, runs through the process of conscious life as we know it. The Idea of the Good is this condition, understood in a generalised sense. Unlike the Ideas of Kinds, it is a condition that results in the production of no one order of beings; but, in virtue of it, interaction among the beings that correspond to the Ideas is brought to pass.

Plotinus, following out the implications of Plato's thought, reaches more metaphysical exactitude. "The Good", he says, is not "good". In itself it is unknowable; but, as the universe for Plato in the *Timaeus* is one, its principle must evidently be one; and so it is identified by Plotinus with the One in the *Parmenides*, pre-eminently in its aspect as unknowable, "the One without predicates". That the Good is beyond or before the essence of actual things[1] means that the reason of the world's existence was that it was good that it should exist. This does not, however, exclude evils, which are a necessity, and, as was said in the *Theaetetus*, cannot be expelled from human life.

According to the Neo-Platonic view, reality is not only One but Many; and for the manifestation of the Many, limitation and imperfection are necessities. In the Scholasticism that became the authorised philosophy of the long and complex succeeding period, the optimism derived from Plotinus and Proclus, and used as an aid against the heretical Manichaeans, is often narrowed to the mere ab-

[1] *Rep.* VI, 509 B: οὐκ οὐσίας ὄντος τοῦ ἀγαθοῦ, ἀλλ' ἔτι ἐπέκεινα τῆς οὐσίας πρεσβείᾳ καὶ δυνάμει ὑπερέχοντος.

stract statement that evil is a negation; but when we
come, after a thousand years, to Nicholas of Cusa,
the first of modern as distinguished from mediaeval
philosophers, we find the revived ancient tradition
putting forth new blossoms. In juxtaposition with,
but in essential detachment from, the theology of
his third book *De Docta Ignorantia*,[1] the fifteenth-
century Cardinal proves that no individual being
can attain perfection in its kind; yet nothing is so imperfect in all respects that there cannot be anything
more imperfect.[2] There is nothing in the universe
that does not enjoy some singularity; and nothing
excels all others in all qualities. Many qualities
exist unknown to us; and of those that are known
men judge according to the diversities of their
religions and their countries. Thus, while "man
does not desire another nature, but only to be

[1] On renewed reading, I am inclined to see in this third book a less
orthodox theology than appears on the surface; but I limit myself to
the philosophical prelude.

[2] *De Docta Ignorantia*, lib. III, cap. I: "Inter plurima etenim eius-
dem speciei individua diversitatem graduum perfectionis cadere
necesse est; quare nullum secundum datam speciem erit maxime per-
fectum, quo perfectius dari non possit, neque etiam adeo imperfectum
est dabile, quod imperfectius dabile non sit. Terminum igitur speciei
nullum attigit".

perfect in his own ",[1] each person must be content
to restrict his aim at perfection not merely within
human limits but within the limits of his individual
nature and of his own nation; admiring nevertheless
the qualities of others; that so there may be unity
and peace without envy.[2]

Through a common error in historical perspec-
tive, we recognise with something of a shock that,
in whatever way we measure the distance, there is
approximately as long a time between Nicholas of
Cusa and Guidano Bruno as between Descartes and
Kant. The names in the two cases mark the difference of spirit between the periods. The watchword
of the seventeenth and eighteenth, as distinguished
from the fifteenth and sixteenth, centuries might have
been, "Back from ontology to theory of knowledge". Spinoza indeed forms an exception; his
aim being still, like that of the thinkers of the Re-
naissance, to grasp the whole. Yet this was pursued
with a care about method which, while it has made
the *Ethics* in style one of the most finished classics of

[1] *De Docta Ignorantia,* lib. ii, cap. 12.
[2] The late modern time is less optimistic in tone than the Renais-
sance. Compare Santayana, *The Life of Reason* ("Reason in Society",
chap. i, p. 28), on "The jumbled context of this world, where the
Fates, like an absent-minded printer, seldom allow a single line to
stand perfect and unmarred".

philosophy, has also limited its range. Interest in
cosmogony, or even in cosmology, and every suggestion of an evolution of the universe or of its parts,
are as completely absent as teleology. Spinoza's
universe is not untruly described as "static". At
the same time, while he takes mathematical physics
as the ideal in seeking explanations of phenomena, his personal attitude to that which is beyond
or behind phenomena is expressed in terms that
have come down from Plotinus. The phrase *amor
intellectualis* can be traced from the ancient to the
modern thinker through a definite series of inter-
mediaries.[1] And, though Spinoza repudiated the
tradition for which Plato and Aristotle were still
authoritative, yet in the enthusiasm inspired in him
by mathematical method he is not essentially remote from Plato himself.

Sir James Jeans, in going back to Plato as the
greatest light of ancient thought, and as still having
a message for the modern world, might have taken
for motto the saying attributed to him in antiquity,
ὁ θεὸς γεωμετρεῖ. Though it is not actually in
Plato, as was well known in the time of Plutarch,

---

[1] I have shown this in detail in an article entitled "Transcendence
in Spinoza" (*Mind*, July, 1929).

there is something in the *Laws* by which it may have been suggested. In a remarkable passage (VII, 818) the "Athenian Stranger" declares that no being who is ignorant of mathematical necessity can be regarded as a god; and with such necessity no god will contend; though the popular saying as to the impossibility of contending with physical necessities is a most foolish one.

Jeans, however, while claiming even more for mathematics than Plato, yet appears, with Spinoza, to leave no theoretical place for the teleology which, as we have just seen by glimpses, forms so conspicuous a part in the doctrines of the Platonic tradition. At the same time, he deviates both from Spinoza and from Plato's Hellenic successors, and probably from Plato himself, in admitting a beginning of the universe. This admission—new to science and alien to the philosophers whose ontology I was most inclined to follow—I had myself arrived at on the strength of what seemed to me compulsory metaphysical arguments. Rather earlier, I had come to the conclusion that biological and psychological evolution requires the restoration of teleology.[1] The

[1] See the articles "Teleology and the Individual" and "A New Metaphysic of Evolution" in the volume entitled *The Metaphysics of Evolution* (1926, re-issued 1928).

result of these developments, which obviously I find reinforced by the newest science, must evidently be a nearer approximation to Platonism as distinguished from Spinozism; for Platonism is less profoundly modified by denial of the infinite past series of events than Spinozism would be by the re-admission of teleology. The *Ethics* of Spinoza, in its combination of intellectual and emotional elements, remains unique as a work of art remains. To feel its power, we no more need to accept it as a total system than we need to accept the theological or atheological systems of Lucretius or Dante or Milton. Where we may still find philosophical inspiration in Spinoza is in the resolute direction of his thought to the problem of Being. He more than any other modern gives renewed encouragement towards an enterprise worthy of a new century if it is ever to find a distinctive way. For the nineteenth century closed without even a provisional solution of any of its larger problems, leaving for the first phase of the twentieth only the ironic comment of events on the faith of its predecessor in perpetual progress.

III

ACCORDING to Jeans, Thought precedes the world; and the pre-mundane Thought of the Universe may be called mathematical "if we can agree that this is to connote the whole of pure thought, and not merely the studies of the professional mathematician".[1] Such an extension of the term would make it include that "dialectic" which Plato ranked before mathematics. It is, as I have noted, Platonic in spirit; and it is the view at which I arrived by attempting successive modifications of the ancient Neo-Platonism as an aid to ontological speculation. The latest results of science, as I have said, came to some extent as a confirmation of my metaphysical reasoning. For the sake of simplicity and brevity, I omit for the moment any reference to the stages by which I arrived at the conclusion, and state the ultimate argument, which I base on Spencer's Universal Postulate, that a proposition of which the

[1] *The Mysterious Universe*, p. 138.

negation is inconceivable must be true.[1] This I take in a more distinctively *a priori* sense than Spencer committed himself to. However attenuated the *a priori* may become, there are, I hold, certain elementary principles that cannot be derived from accumulated experiences, even of the race, but are arrived at by analysis as axioms, whether of formal inference, of mathematical deduction, or of natural and humanistic science. The appropriate analysis proves in each case that if thought, be it general or more or less specialised, is to proceed, we cannot do without them.

The proposition which I assert is: "that the number of all singly numerable[2] things and events, present and past, is finite".

No one, I think, will deny that, so far as arguments from experience can establish a generalised statement about the universe, the recent advances of

[1] *The Principles of Psychology*, vol. II, part vii, chap. 11.
[2] This expression, chosen to bar out recourse to the notion of real infinitesimals as a means of defending the "actual infinite", I was glad to find perfectly conformable to the position decisively taken up by Prof. Whitehead (*Process and Reality*, Part IV, chap. v, § 4, p. 465): "In mathematics, all phraseology about infinitesimals is merely disguised statement about a class of finites". This he declares to be now the authorised doctrine of mathematicians.

astronomical science have tended to confirm the view to which this proposition leads. With its distances calculated in "light-years", the new astronomy arouses a far more vivid imagination of immensity than could ever be awakened by the vague thought of infinite space; but it no longer leaves open the possibility that any actual body should travel in a Euclidean straight line without limit; and, if accepted physical inferences are not wrong, it points back to a temporal beginning of the whole aggregate of stellar systems.

In attempting a further development, I must first observe that nothing gives me so strong an impression of the power of the human mind as the achievements of mathematical physics, and especially of astronomy. But the metaphysician, admiring from a distance, ought always to remember Hume's warning that he cannot emulate the procedure of the mathematical sciences; he must beware of long trains of deductive reasoning when applied to his own subjects, which do not admit of similar precautions against ambiguous terms. Yet astronomy and physics do not exhaust the Whole.

For example, to reach positions like those of

Jeans and Eddington, who find the beginning of things in Thought, mathematical science requires the aid of idealistic theory of knowledge, which in the series of the sciences immediately follows psychology and not mathematics. A "subjective" science, coming last, is thus needed to interpret the first, which is the basis of all the "objective" sciences. Not that the character of mathematics itself does not make an important difference when interpreted. Hume, in his *Dialogues concerning Natural Religion*, arrived at the conclusion, in which, he maintained, the Theist and the Atheist must agree, *That the cause or causes of order in the universe probably bear some remote analogy to human intelligence.* Now this proposition, in itself, has some ambiguity; for "intelligence" may be taken either on its sentient or on its rational side; but undoubtedly the argument of Jeans, that nature could not be so well interpreted in terms of a science which, like mathematics, springs almost unmixedly from human reason, if it were not that something like mathematical thought is realised in nature, tends to fix the analogy on the side of intellect distinctively so called, rather than on the side of a diffused sentiency as that which is concealed or revealed by natural things. And, as Spinoza said, if the analogy to the human mind is permissible, then the intellect of the Whole must proceed in exactly the opposite way to that which we know in our own mental history as individuals; that is to say, it must proceed not from the things of experience to thought, but from thought to things.

It is in such expressions that Spinoza Platonises; and from this point we may turn back to Plotinus and Proclus, who, if not more cosmogonic, were at least more cosmologic than the inheritor of their rationalist metaphysics in the seventeenth century. Now I find that, in my first attempt to show how there might still be a distinctive truth in their theory of the universe,[1] I was partly wrong and partly right. The theory, deduced from their form of idealistic metaphysics, that the Whole, since it has existed as a necessary manifestation of Mind without limit in

[1] *The Neo-Platonists*, "Conclusion". As this Conclusion marked a definite dialectical stage, I deliberately refrained from revising it in the later editions. In "Teleology and the Individual" I was still at the same stage. The modification was made in "A New Metaphysic of Evolution".

Of course this refers entirely to hypothetical applications to distinctively modern problems, which I have kept quite separate from the exposition of the Neo-Platonists themselves.

the past, must always remain in its general aspect the same, cannot indeed be upheld in face of the new astronomy; but the metaphysical doctrine in its purity can be applied even more effectively than it was by themselves as a ground for the unity of the universe. For if the universe has a total evolution in time, it is distinctly more "one"—more unitary— in accordance with its Cause, than if, as I suggested, it consists of many systems analogous to our solar system, all simultaneously at various stages of cyclical movement. I must add that I still cherish a certain scepticism as to the Second Law of Thermo-dynamics. Its necessary rejection by their doctrine was something of an attraction. Is not this law, as some men of science have asked, unscientifically anthropomorphic in its statement? Has the "avail-ability" of energy, which can be shown to be per-petually diminishing in the material universe as now known, any meaning except in relation to the present purposes of man? Jeans himself, discussing the question about the element of apparent in-determination in physical processes, argues that apparently accidental events may be as completely determined as those that we can, with our existing knowledge, assign to known causes; since they may depend on causes within the Whole that are unknown to us.[1] Does not this suggest that, at some phase in the universal process, the "law of entropy" may, through the passing into act of causes hitherto latent in the metaphysical Whole, lose its supposed validity as a formula for everlasting time? Thus there may after all be an immortal universe, as the Neo-Platonists held.

There remains also a kind of infinity of space and time belonging really to the mind which imposes them as its "forms". Empty space cannot be imagined as curved; and time as well as space is subjectively infinite; that is to say, imagination inevitably transcends any limit assigned to space or time. In time, what has to be thought as finite is the series of past events; in space, the number of bodies or the extension of the ether—whatever the ether may be. What the "meta-mathematicians" did in preparation for Einstein's Theory of Relativity was not to show that empty space in abstraction can be figured as other than homaloidal and infinite, but that various hypotheses can be worked out sym-

[1] *The Mysterious Universe*, p. 125.

bolically as regards the plenum of extension. This, it now appears, is probably such that, if a traveller could set out on a journey of cosmic dimensions in what appears to us as a straight line, something that we may call for convenience an ethereal medium would so constrain the traveller's movements that after a very long time he would arrive from the opposite side at the spot whence he had set out. The constraint has caused his path to deviate from what we still imagine as a Euclidean straight line cutting through the medium. Thus we arrive at Einstein's formula that the world is for all possible motions "finite but boundless". The infinity of the universe of matter is an illusion that was made and can be unmade by the human mind.

Pre-mundane Thought, in which the possibility, which is also the necessity, of the universe in evolution is prefigured, is necessarily absolute (or complete) and infinite (because there is nothing to bound it). It must also be conceived as one and eternal. But perhaps there is here too much defini- tion. Ought we not to say with Plotinus that the One is beyond Intellect? For in the beginning of the world-process not only intellect, but also what the

5-2

psychologists call feeling and will, must be supposed latent. On this, paradoxically, an argument might be founded for personalising the Absolute and Infinite. As there is something unknowable in a personality, with its elements of will and feeling which come to light in the course of individual development, may there not also be something resembling personality in the unknowable? This would become more known as the universe evolves. Another paradox would follow: that the One, as the Neo-Platonists said, does not "know itself"— or at least we cannot say that it does—but produces self-knowing intellect at the next stage. Personality, however, conveys so much the notion of finitude and relativity that I prefer to say that the Principle of the Whole must be super-personal. Still, I agree with Bradley that it is of real importance to view the ultimate metaphysical principle as comparable (if comparison is permitted) to personal mind rather than to something that we know only as sub-personal. This would apply to analogies with Instinct; which is properly, though always requiring a modicum of intelligence to work it, a kind of subsidiary mechanism preserved for its utility in the struggle for existence. An achieved "intuition", such as Spinoza's *scientia intuitiva*, which goes beyond experience and discursive reason, is at the other extreme. It is from this, and not from some *Élan vital*, that we attain, in Spinoza's view, most insight into the reality of the universe. And, at the culminating point of his *Ethics*, he makes the minds that comprehend the universal order and feel joy in the comprehension "eternal modes" of Infinite Intellect.

This is a height from which, when it has been reached, descent is difficult. Mathematics gives us no help. Putting the question as to an end for the universe, Jeans observes that organic life, with its quantitative insignificance, has not the look of being a result at which the Whole can be conceived to aim. In the immense expanse of which no account can be given save that every process in it conforms to mathematical law, human life seems an insignificant accident.

Organic life, however, exists; and, if we are to argue simply from what we know, it is a defensible position that the mathematical laws, in any sense intelligible to us, would not exist if there were not minds at the human level to grasp them. A possible view is that the universe is aiming at consciousness of itself and partly attains its end in man. Going, perhaps, beyond his earlier theoretical system, Comte even argued that, if there is to be the smallest real existence, it is rigorously necessary that there should be at least one world in which there is contemplation of it.[1]

I propose, however, to bring down the argument to something below the cosmic level, and to deal distinctively with the problem of the Many, which I make no attempt to deduce from the One.

Whether they are real or not, there are at any rate apparent "final causes" in the life of organisms. An organism, animal or vegetable, acts as if it had, primarily, the purpose of self-conservation. Bacon's and Descartes' rule of ignoring final causes in scientific investigation was not found to be practicable in the case of organisms. Whether a biologist is in philosophy a "mechanicist" or a "vitalist", he does, in physiology, carry on his researches with a view to finding out the apparent purpose which each organ subserves. Now all processes may take

[1] *Système de Politique Positive*, t. 1, p. 439.

place in accordance with physico-chemical laws, and we may agree with the mechanicists in rejecting everything of the nature of a "vital force" or "vital energy" classifiable with the other forces or energies of nature; but one question remains insoluble. Can it be conceived that, at a definable phase in the movements of particles, a formula in mathematico-physical or physico-chemical terms shall emerge from which an expert can infer at a glance that here precisely the reality of the calculated paths of the particles will take on the illusory disguise of purpose? If this is chimerical, then clearly the teleological nature of an organism must be accepted as something which, though it may be analysed through and through in terms of the sciences preliminary to biology, cannot be predicted as a total phenomenon of nature from anything simpler that precedes it.

Actually it is the experts in the preliminary sciences, with their knowledge of what mathematico-physical explanation really means, who have usually seen this most clearly. By others, "mechanical" is often used in a vague sense as meaning nothing more than "in accordance with scientific law". But Comte, who was by training a mathematician, found that the distinctive actions of an organism are cases of a special class of scientific laws expressible only in teleological terms; and pointed out (as E. Mach did later) that the accepted laws of motion, in various statable cases, fail to determine without ambiguity the direction of motion of a particle. I do not myself see how to put the result in any less metaphysical way than that something which we may call the "teleological idea" of the organism determines the direction of a motion otherwise ambiguous.

This teleological idea I take to be part of a pre-existent Many. In some sense, the metaphysical universe is larger than the physical. That is to say, the physical universe, as mentally constructed from data of sight and touch, is not fully representative of all the real causes that exist. Some of these causes, passing out of latency from age to age, manifest themselves biologically in the purposive movements of organisms. On this supposition, the world of organic life may be a directed phase of a process destined to prepare for human thought, by which at length all past causes, from those of astro-physics onward, are grasped. If our earth, as Jeans thinks possible, is the only inhabited body in the universe, then for the sake of this planet of ours all the inanimate bodies, so far as they are really inanimate and so far as we can conceive of any purpose, exist. Should all the multitude of stars, with their formidable magnitudes and distances and radiant energies, seem a large expenditure for such an end, two replies are open according to the mood of the contemplator: either, it was easy for the Cause to produce them; or, "tantae molis erat" to found the human race. As Jeans says about his own suggested mathematical idealism: "It is probably unnecessary to add that, on this view of things, the apparent vastness and emptiness of the universe, and our own insignificant size therein, need cause us neither bewilderment nor concern".[1]

But how are we to interpret the Many which we regard as pre-existent in idea? Here, I think, the right term was supplied by Schopenhauer in his imperfectly worked out theory of "the *aseitas* of the individual". This term he borrowed from the Scholastics to convey the notion of the uncreated,

[1] *The Mysterious Universe*, p. 143.

that which is not merely by itself (*per se*) but from itself (*a se*). Only through this teleological idea of the individual, as we may call it at its most determinate stage,[1] do good and evil manifest themselves in the cosmic process. These conceptions have no place in mathematics, but become indispensable in the transition from biology to psychology, where pleasure and pain appear, with reproduction or destruction of that which seeks to preserve itself.

In a famous passage in the tenth book of the *Laws*, Plato (as Burnet explains it) finds that there must be in the universe at least one soul that is potentially maleficent, and that this cannot be the soul of the Whole. A plurality of souls—some, not merely one —no doubt is meant; but plurality is not said to be the source of evil. Much as he may wish to minimise the admission of real evil as distinguished from error in the human race, Plato evidently found that

---

[1] Having made the transition from "organism" to "individual" without special remark, I must note that Aristotle, in the first book of the *De Anima*, distinguished them, under his concept of "soul", with an accuracy little emulated by the moderns. In the case of vegetables, and of animals that can repair themselves and go on separately when cut in two, he seems to find that there is a soul of the species but not of the individual. Aristotle's "soul" is not quite the same as "teleological idea", but to a certain extent the conceptions coincide.

he must recognise the existence of a few radically unjust and malevolent and at the same time powerful wills. Neither Schopenhauer nor the Neo-Platonists are so explicit as regards the existence of uncreated intrinsic evil; but the Neo-Platonists, as well as Schopenhauer in his later stage, have the notion of an intrinsically differing Many. Out of this, according to Neo-Platonism, conflict necessarily arises; and evil, though in the long run subordinated to good, is an inevitable result of conflict. In accordance with this general view, it might be said, not indeed that all things (when life had begun) were very good, but that they are directed towards good. The individual will remains, but is educable by the process. In a modern form I find the same type of thought in Whitehead's "philosophy of organism". That philosophy I can accept in spirit if I may borrow a phrase from Vico (applied to the Roman law) and describe it as a "severe poem", in which systems of destiny, realised in races, religions, political communities, and finally in individuals, are all complicated into a total, not wholly inscrutable, evolution of the universe towards ends.

I put my own view in a very generalised form as

follows. Certain teleological ideas of species and of individuals pass from possibility to actuality in such an order of concomitance and succession as to bring to their highest degree the powers of intellect, feeling and will in the consciousness of Truth, Beauty and Goodness.

The triple end of the process, though not the evolutionary theory of its accomplishment, was fixed by Kant in the tripartite division of mind which he took over from the contemporary psychologist J. N. Tetens, and in the titles of his three Critiques, by which he co-ordinated, as the supreme philosophical disciplines, Theory of Knowledge, Aesthetics and Ethics. His triad had indeed been adumbrated before, and incidentally, though never in definitive terms, put into words. In spite of attempted new departures by the voluntarist psychology, which, following a Neo-Scholastic reaction of some time back in Germany,[1] denies the

---

[1] The position formulated in the new departure referred to is "that emotions can be distinguished from each other only by differences in their conative ingredients—that there is no difference between the feeling-tone of one emotion and that of another" (see *Mind*, January, 1930, p. 116). Its Neo-Scholastic anticipation, inspired by "confident attachment to the science of the thirteenth century", is to be found in two books noticed in *Mind*, October, 1885, p. 623: *Das*

co-ordinate rank of Feeling with Thought and Will, and so threatens to blot out Aesthetics, I am content to accept the Kantian formulation as it has established itself in the modern European consciousness.

But if such are the ends, and there is a process leading to them, it does not follow that the movement goes on continuously without break. The history of every civilisation—that of European civilisation most of all—shows that it does not. No one who looks at the facts can admit that every succeeding age is one of improvement in all things; and most of those who think would agree with Mr Aldous Huxley that the advancement of applied science has not been an unmixed good. "Incidentally", as he says,[1] "the progress of science and industry has enormously increased the element of foolery and sordidness in human life." Against this, however, we have to set the light thrown by theoretical science on the highest questions; and per-

Gemüth und das Gefühlsvermögen der neueren Psychologie, by Dr Joseph Jungmann, S.J., and *Grundlinien zur Aristotelisch-Thomistischen Psychologie*, by Dr Vincenz Knauer. What the authors desired to preserve was the element of realism and dualism lost in the modern purely psychological classification.

[1] *Do What You Will*, p. 288.

haps the conditions for the establishment even of logical or mathematical truths are to be found only in what Mr Bertrand Russell calls "this higgledy-piggledy job-lot of a world in which chance has imprisoned us". We may, with Mr Russell,[1] oppose to everything empirical propositions true "in all possible worlds"; but, after all, the possible worlds are in ourselves, and the thought of them has come to us from the existing universe. For the Whole, considered metaphysically and not as an abstraction such as that Nature which is regarded as excluding Man, produced ourselves and all our ideals. The poets may make Prometheus defy Zeus, and we may enjoy the representation without afterthought; for it brings before us one aspect of life; but ultimately they themselves know that "harsh Gods and hostile Fates are dreams".

A fact to give cause for reflection is that, of all philosophers, the pessimists have put forth what are most unmistakably theodicies. There is of course in Schopenhauer much more than pessimism; but it was as an avowed pessimist that he professed a doctrine showing the way to the final deliverance of

[1] *Introduction to Mathematical Philosophy* (1919), chap. XVII, p. 192.

the individual from evil. The way lies in extinction of the "will to live"; for this, appropriate systems of discipline have been evolved; but destiny has to give its aid. His disciples, Hartmann and Main-länder, went further; not being content with the redemption of the individual if the whole world also could not be redeemed.

For Hartmann, the world began with a lapse of the Unconscious into consciousness; but this same Unconscious has devised a world-process for its own liberation. At last, by a collective act of will, when the illusion of happiness has been seen through, the human race, its highest product, will cause the Whole to return to an unconscious repose not to be broken again through all eternity.

Hartmann himself, like Schopenhauer, found the present life very tolerable, and theorised on the mode of conduct that is a serviceable compromise for those who are unable to become saints. Main-länder was a more consistent pessimist,—in fact, the most consistent known; and his doctrine, though he declared himself the first to have demonstrated Atheism scientifically, was most of all a theodicy. In his view, the pre-mundane unity, which he calls

God, aiming at self-annihilation but unable to achieve it all at once, broke up into individuals and set going the "struggle for existence" so that they might wear each other down, till at last the end, which is "absolute death", is attained by all. The destined "way of the world to not-being" is the ghost of the "dead godhead".

Mainländer's historical affinities were displayed in a fragment of autobiography which appeared in 1898. "If we still lived in the Middle Ages", he confessed, "I know perfectly well that I should become a Carthusian monk."[1] He ended by suicide as soon as he knew that his *Philosophy of Redemption* had been sent into the world for its emancipation. He had undoubtedly something of philosophical genius; and his work has a special point of interest for present cosmogonical theories. Apparently without knowledge of the scientific law, he anticipated metaphysically the doctrine of "entropy". The world-process, he said, will finally cease through the "weakening of force"—a deeper

[1] This is given in a contribution by Dr Fritz Sommerlad of Giessen to the *Zeitschrift für Philosophie und philosophische Kritik*, Bd. 112, pp. 74–101.

law than the "conservation of force"; and in the knowledge of this and of his own approaching extinction the individual may achieve beatitude.

A passing speculation of Jeans, to the effect that life may be a temporary phenomenon of the "running down" of matter, has some resemblance to this result; though we are not asked to salute it with joy. How little the type of our physical theory can determine about reality becomes clear when we turn from a pessimist of the nineteenth century to an optimist of the ninth. John Scotus Erigena, near the end of his *De Divisione Naturae*, imagines a final dissolution of the physical universe in a manner not unlike that which is supposed by the modern cosmogonists who predict the disappearance of all matter into radiation. The difference is that Erigena does not make individual life and thought come to an end, but holds that they go on in the perfect harmony of a purely mental universe which has taken up into itself the whole reality of the past.

Having become as clear as Eddington, for example, is among men of science, that physics cannot as such be an ontology, we may go on to consider more definitely the question whether there is anything perdurable in what we have called the teleological idea of the individual. Is not the individual, it may be asked, entirely a product of something more general? It may be granted that, as Nicholas of Cusa said, absolute equality excludes individuality. Each individual, to be such, must differ in some degree from all the rest. But cannot "the individual", whether thing or person, arise as a complex of elements that admit of all sorts of permutations, or else as a segregated portion of some substance that is the basis of the world? In either case, individuals would begin and end; being either resolved into their elements or reabsorbed into the Whole. Why suppose anything of the nature of a pre-existent idea?

These questions I have tried to answer in the essays, "Teleology and the Individual" and "A New Metaphysic of Evolution".[1] I will briefly recapitulate my positions.

It must be remembered that I am trying to assign causes which are at the same time reasons, causes in the ancient sense (αἰτίαι); *i.e.*, the metaphysical

[1] *The Metaphysics of Evolution*, Part II.

causes that Comte expelled from his Positive Philosophy. To arrive at metaphysical causes, in my view,
we must work with terms that have a psychological
meaning. If we bring in electrons, for example, we
must consider ourselves as dealing, not with the un-
representable units that mathematicians make the
object of their symbolism, but with psychical correlates of these. Can we derive a psychical individual
from the correlates, in this "subjective" sense, of
electrons? The simple but conclusive answer to this
is that mere coexistences and sequences of feelings do
not of themselves become relations in a consciousness. A unitary consciousness has to be presupposed:
its origin cannot be explained from associated elements.

As causal explanation the possibility is thus excluded, either that consciousness is an accident of
myriads of undetermined collocations of billions of
electrons, or that it is the work of an Artificer putting
together similar billions in accordance with a
mathematical plan. The execution of the plan might,
in accordance with the old theory of "occasional
causes", serve as the cue to some "daemon" to set
the mechanism going; but Hume disposed for

ever of the notion that there is here any properly rational ground to go upon in inferring anything.

But cannot an individual consciousness be explained as a differentiation from a kind of universal sentiency, correlated with what we call material objects, and consisting of feelings already related? The reply was indicated in antiquity by some unknown thinker whose argument became current in the schools.[1] If individual souls could be produced by differentiation from the soul of the Whole, then, by analogy, consciousness as known in ourselves and others should show itself capable of producing new minds by a sort of budding off such as takes place in organisms. But we have no experience of this. Individual consciousness arises anew in the growth of new organisms, not directly from pre-existing minds.[2] If experimental psychologists can tell us about phenomena of double or multiple personality, we may reply that these are not cases in which a new soul, so to speak, goes off by itself like the result of

[1] It was preserved by Joannes Philoponus. See *The Metaphysics of Evolution*, Part II, Appendix, p. 461, note.

[2] I am here slightly expanding the ancient writer's argument.

the division of a protozoon. The diverse "personalities" arise from temporary suppressions (correlated no doubt with some physiological modification in the organism) of elements in a maximum personality which can sometimes be redintegrated by curative agencies—say, psycho-analysis or hypnotism. I do not at least know of any cases in which, apart from exceptionally vivid dramatisation, a new soul is apparently brought to coexist in the same body with the original tenant. We all experience "dissociated activities"; and it seems impossible to say, *a priori*, how far pathological exaggerations of these may go.

Moreover, the relation between any two minds is in one way quite unlike the relation between the corresponding bodies. The two bodies are distinctly marked off from one another as portions of extension. The corresponding two minds have no boundary; while at the same time each contains in its thought the universe, including its own body.[1]

I do not say that such considerations demonstrate

[1] I quote again, as I have quoted on other occasions, Arist. *De An.* III, 8, 431 b 21: ἡ ψυχὴ τὰ ὄντα πώς ἐστι πάντα.

the pre-existence and perdurability of "ideas of individuals"; but I do say that the way in which individual minds can either grow or be put together from psychical elements or from a "ground", or can be dissolved or re-absorbed, has not yet been shown in intelligible terms. The appearances leave us with nothing but "occasional causes", or Hume's expectations founded on customary conjunctions, or the shadows on the wall of the "Platonic cave". We are at liberty to make hypotheses. The hypothesis I have put forth is that metaphysical beings, hitherto latent, find the way to manifest themselves when the real processes correlated with physical change have made phenomena possible that could not be produced earlier. One manifestation of the pre-existent Many is in the lives of animals, culminating in human life.

This theory has an obvious resemblance to the "monadic" hypothesis of Leibniz; but I think that, by going back to earlier sources for suggestions, I have cleared it of the special Leibnizian apparatus of "windowless" monads and "pre-established harmony", which depended essentially on the effort to carry through, consistently with the idealism which

Leibniz professed,[1] the doctrine that, corresponding to every psychical process, there is a thoroughgoing order of mechanical causation complete within itself. By preserving only the essence of Leibniz's theory as applied to minds, we rid ourselves of the successive degenerations of the theory of psychophysical parallelism;[2] first into "Animal Automatism", which treated the sequence of feelings in men and animals alike as having no influence on their actions; and finally into contemporary

[1] Lettre I à M. Remond de Montmort: "que les *Monades*, ou les substances simples, sont les seules véritables substances; et que les choses matérielles ne sont que des phénomènes, mais bien fondés et bien liés".

[2] The most philosophical form of the doctrine of "parallelism" was that of Spinoza, applied to the two attributes of Substance as conceived by him, viz., Thought and Extension. Leibniz, in taking it over, gave it a highly artificial turn, but beneath this it had the same scientific implications. Thought was not in theory subordinated to Extension; as it was not in the doctrine of the man of genius who founded the new science of Psycho-physics, G. T. Fechner. The result, however, of the working out of physiological psychology in the laboratory has been to disappoint the hopes, cherished by Fechner himself, of new light on metaphysics. Psycho-physics remains simply one of the minor positive sciences that have branched off from psychology as a philosophical science; and psychologists seem to be discovering that, when applied, it has done little more than show how, by directing mental attention, the human organism can be mechanised in a great variety of ways.

"Behaviourism", which treats the external actions as alone existent.

Taking the *Monadology* and the brief *Commentatio de Anima Brutorum* as the standards of reference, I have no difficulty in accepting what Leibniz says about the inner nature of his monads. It is agreeable to note that he definitely repudiated the repellent notion, attributed to him in his own time, that the psychical reality of an organism is the dominance of a ruling soul or monad over a hierarchy of servant-monads each with a kind of consciousness of its own, in virtue of which it obeys orders from above.[1] Points independent of all his special apparatus are: that perception cannot be explained from mechanical motion of particles; that if we are to speak of human souls we must also speak of animal souls, and that these too must be regarded as "indefectible"; that any possible basis for holding that human souls are "immortal" as distinguished from merely indefectible (that is, as an ancient thinker would have said, "ingenerable and indestructible") consists in their power of conceptual thought and of memory. By this last we must of course understand not the

[1] *La Monadologie* (ed. Erdmann), § 71.

mere power to identify places and persons, which is not peculiar to man, but the power to assign memories to an order of sequent events, for which physiological psychology, in the opinion of some accomplished psychologists, has so far failed to show any conceivable basis in nervous process. An essential part of the doctrine is also that there are not separated souls (animas separatas naturaliter[1] non dari); though perhaps we might speak, on Leibnizian principles, of "separable souls", if we mean only that "teleological ideas of individuals" may continue to exist in a latent state without actual phenomenal manifestation.

Having paid this tribute to the great representative in modern times of the belief in metaphysical individuality, I may observe that Schopenhauer's term *aseitas* has an advantage over *monas* in so far as it indicates the impossibility of deriving the inmost nature of the individual from anything outside itself. Aristotle, it is noteworthy, rejected the term

[1] "Naturaliter" was no doubt inserted by Leibniz to avoid possible objection by theologians. "Supernaturally" there might be separated souls. Critics have noted that Leibniz, while thinking as a philosopher, never lost the pre-occupation with what might be thought of his positions by the religious authorities.

monas for the soul on the ground that each soul must have a difference from others; and that the notion of a unit, or of a "unitary point", does not convey the idea of a difference.[1] Perhaps when the biochemists have arrived at the limits of their success as architects of organisms moulded to some ideal of social "efficiency", the infrangible individual being that has baffled them may be restored by later science under the name of the *archeus* of an older physiology. No age has known better than the present that earlier scientific hypotheses, disused for a time, have a way of coming back, not indeed precisely in their ancient guise, but with fresh renewal of their "winter weeds outworn".

To discard the view that the monads are "windowless" implies that we do not take the process in which the individual being is manifested to be a purely internal "evolution", in the meaning that the word had in the time of Leibniz. In terms of evolution in its later sense, the monads act and are acted on by the real being of the world (however

[1] *De An.* I, 4, 409 a 18: ἐνδέχεται δὲ δή πῶς μονάδα ταύτην εἶναι; δεῖ γὰρ ὑπάρχειν τινὰ αὐτῇ διαφορὰν πρὸς τὰς ἄλλας. στιγμῆς δὲ μοναδικῆς τίς ἂν εἴη διαφορὰ πλὴν θέσις; (I follow the reading in Biehl's edition.)

this may be conceived) and are modified in the process; so that there is necessarily the appearance of interaction with phenomena. Leibniz himself held that there is a kind of "selection". Selected monads go on from the stage of merely sensitive to that of rational souls possessing the kind of memory that accompanies reason. Here we may easily find a suggestion of a psychological, as well as biological, evolution of species. To the "teleological idea of the individual", there is therefore no difficulty in supposing that there is added, at a higher stage, what Aristotle called "separable intellect" (νοῦς χωριστός); that is, intellect without organic correlate, though not, of course, out of relation to the mental factors, such as perception and imagination, that *have* an organic correlate. And, in his *Matière et Mémoire*, Bergson has revived the theory of Plotinus that there arises in the course of life a memory separable from brain-activity; though, as in the case of the Aristotelian separable intellect, not disconnected, during the life of the body, from the psychical factors related to that life.

Insensibly I have passed on to points that Leibniz could not have admitted consistently with his "pre-established harmony", which required complete correlation of mental and mechanical processes; but, as has been seen, the positions are far from being entirely novel. If we were to accept them all—survival of teleological idea, of thought and of memory —then, since personality is unitary, we should have to add, with an echo of a well-known formula: "and yet there are not three separables, but one separable". Plotinus seems to have allowed the separability in all three cases; but other philosophers have taken a more limited view. Schopenhauer, in his later years, believed in some undefined *palingenesia* of the "will to live"; even saying that he "should not attain nirvana", not being yet fit for it. The intellect and memory acquired by the individual he probably conceived as not going on to a new life. Proclus, for whom the permanence of the individual reason was a certainty, does not express himself definitely about memory; but adds to the pure reason, which according to Aristotle is immortal, what he describes as roots of the "irrational soul": in virtue of these, the individual is permanently differentiated. Comparable to the doctrine of Proclus is that of one Christian theologian. Aiming at a transformation of "the resurrection of the body", to meet the attacks of pagans who treated it as repulsive materialism, he put forward the subtle theory that it really means a reincarnation, not from the particles of the former body, but from a λόγος latent in it. Since Origen did not admit that any new state of the world can ever precisely resemble any former state, this was a decided improvement on the doctrine of the Stoics, whose recurrent cycles were never to result in anything but an exact repetition of the course of the world, and of every individual life, as they have been in our own cosmic period. If Leibniz had taken up Origen's general conception, he might have made of it something comparable to modern evolution; but in the *Théodicée* he deliberately set it aside in favour of the doctrine of more orthodox theologians.

Questions about the future of mind or minds, I hope I have at least shown, are not capable of any facile solution. My own opinion is that, though unsolved, they are not necessarily insoluble. If they are ever to be brought nearer to a solution, it cannot be without the aid of physiological science; but at present the problem seems to be to gain for ourselves a certain freedom of thinking as against a mechanicist dominance which has sometimes shown itself little less than a rival orthodoxy. Freedom has been achieved in astronomy; but, as Jeans tells us, a star is a much simpler thing than an organism. We must not, therefore, think the most important questions are solved because we know so much about the magnitudes, distances, composition and temperature of the stars. Importance and unimportance are not physical concepts to be fixed by quantitative estimates. Apart from teleology, they have for us no meaning. No doubt there is a certain audacity in applying teleology to the cosmos; but we know at any rate that stars came before organisms in evolution, and these before mind as manifested in man. If we treat this order of "genesis" as fundamentally teleological, then the ultimate importance of cosmogony is that it shows how the way is prepared for organisms; organisms themselves being of importance only as means to the manifestation of mind.[1] Of minds, once manifested, not merely the organism but the whole universe must be conceived as the vehicle. Individual

[1] As Proclus quotes from Theophrastus: οὐδὲν τίμιον ἄνευ ψυχῆς.

minds, as has been already seen, we must suppose
to have been latent as necessities in pre-mundane
Thought. And, to understand how the actual universe was possible, we must assume a pre-existent
Many as well as One.

A problem, slightly touched in passing, remains,
which is ultimately a question for philosophic
thought, and in which science cannot give the final
decision. Determinism, it will scarcely be denied, is
an ideal for science, since it simply means that
nothing in the whole world escapes causation. Yet
it cannot be proved by science, which would not be
rendered unworkable in practice by real exceptions;
as it is not ruined by inability to calculate in particular cases. And in fact we now find, among adepts
in the exact sciences, a disposition to bring back indeterminism in the form of a kind of Epicurean
clinamen. The electrons, in the new physics, may
deviate without assignable cause, like the atoms of
Epicurus. From the point of view of pure science as
of formal logic, therefore, it seems impossible to
frame a stringent proof that such elements of
"chance and spontaneity", as Aristotle had called
them (perhaps not without influence on Epicurus),

are not part of the universe. They may, then, form part of human action; and in this some find hope. My own attitude is the opposite. Ethically, indeterminism suggests to me nothing but malign Chance; whereas beneficent Fortune always suggests causation. Thus I feel in myself no repugnance to a well-known stanza of Omar Khayyam, almost literally equivalent to the lines in the *Oedipus* of Seneca:

> Omnia secto tramite vadunt,
> Primusque dies dedit extremum.

There is, however, a real "fallacy of Fatalism", dependent on the illusory imagination that decisions of the individual have no part in the course of events, but that the Whole as such causes every act, so that all will go in the same way whatever the individual may decide. The "freedom" of the individual, if we may use the term as against fatalism, consists in its *aseitas*, not in the absence of necessity. As Plotinus pointed out, correcting some exaggerations of the Stoics, to treat every action of every person as simply an effect of the constraint of the Whole, employing each will as an agent, is, by an excess of causation, to destroy the possibility of tracing out any relations of cause and effect in the detail of actual events.

My ascription of determinism to Plotinus is the one point on which Dean Inge finds that he cannot agree with my exposition. I recognise that it is a very subtle determinism; even more so than that of Kant and Schopenhauer; but perhaps the term has come to suggest too strongly a thoroughgoing mechanicism. Teleological causation, however, seems to me equally to come under the head of determinism. I am unable to see any antithesis between causation and teleology. For Leibniz, the principle behind all laws of causation is the teleological "principle of sufficient reason". Though this was not so for Hume, he yet rejected, as Leibniz might have done, all distinction in principle between the "necessity" we find in the motions of inanimate bodies and in the actions of human beings. In both cases, according to Hume, what is psychologically behind the conviction of necessity is only an expectation following on the uniformity of conjunctions in experience. This expectation, he shows, is often stronger in the case of human beings than in the case of external things. An illustration is given in almost the same words in the *Treatise* and in the *Inquiry*: "A prisoner who has neither money nor interest, discovers the impossibility of his escape, as well when he considers the obstinacy of the gaoler, as the walls and bars with which he is surrounded; and, in all attempts for his freedom, chooses rather to work upon the stone and iron of the one, than upon the inflexible nature of the other".[1] What this seems to me to prove is that we are more firmly convinced of necessity in proportion as we understand it more from within. And the reason, the αἰτία, is more understood thus in the case of a "final" than of an "efficient" cause.

For Spinoza, the type of necessity was that which is seen most of all from within, viz., logical or mathematical deduction. This sometimes has the effect of bringing his determinism (like that of the Stoics, though theirs was teleological) rather close in appearance to fatalism. For example, there is the proposition (*Eth.* IV, Prop. 54) that all *poenitentia* is

---

[1] I have transcribed the sentence from Selby-Bigge's edition of the *Inquiry* (Sect. VIII, Part I: "Of Liberty and Necessity". Cf. *Treatise*, Book II, Sect. i).

irrational; that any one who repents—that is, allows himself to dwell on feelings of regret—becomes twice (instead of only once) impotent or miserable. Mr J. M. Robertson has well put the objection when he says:[1] "Unless by *poenitentia* Spinoza meant self-punishment (as, scourging) his proposition would seem fitted to recommend itself solely to the quite non-moral man—Iago or Borgia or Richard". The possible reply had occurred to me that "extremes meet": the "free man" of Spinoza, who lives by the dictate of reason without passion, and "the quite non-moral man", agree in acquiescing unperturbed in all the consequences of the natural order, whether they themselves have had a part in working it out or not; for in either case it was certain. I agree, however, with Mr Robertson both in rejecting this as an ideal to be set up, and in holding determinism, rationally understood, not to be responsible for it. Since in normal human beings repentance (both egoistic and altruistic) arises of necessity, this necessity also must be endured; and, when brought into clear consciousness, may have value for the conduct of life and for the formation

[1] *A Short History of Morals*, p. 248.

of character, which is one of the things that depend on us.

In Spinoza the overstrain after imperturbability arose no doubt from the traditional claim which Dean Inge has noted in the philosophies of antiquity, above all in Stoicism, that by the practice of them we can "make ourselves invulnerable". We moderns, on the whole, know that this is impossible; and Spinoza himself was so far from succeeding in the aim that he had to be forcibly prevented from losing his life in a public protest of grief and indignation against a political crime.

The most characteristic mood, however, in Spinoza is that in which he goes beyond the Stoics, with their too preponderant "driving at practice". To put joy, finally, above sorrow, Spinoza placed at the summit of his system the theoretic life. Happiness is to be found in contemplating the eternal order of the universe. Now this kind of happiness, of course, has not been the result exclusively of Spinoza's doctrine. And Spinoza himself did not make joy exclusively the accompaniment of the highest achievements of human thought. As the usual sign, in contrast to sorrow, of the passage to a greater perfection, it had a larger reach. Though Spinoza is not so minute as Plato in the *Philebus* in the proof that pure knowledge without any feeling of pleasure, or even knowledge with only the pleasure that necessarily accompanies it, and without any other, is not enough to constitute a human life that can be the object of desire, he agrees in principle. He might even have found that Plato in the *Gorgias*, where the succession of monasticism to Caesarism seems to be prefigured in the speeches of Callicles and the refutations of Socrates, praises abstinence too much. And here it is interesting to find the reasoning of Spinoza on the geometrical model confirmed by the paradoxical wisdom of a modern Gnostic like Blake, for whom reasoning, as distinguished from the intuition of the seer, was the path of error. "Some say that Happiness is not Good for Mortals, and they ought to be answer'd that Sorrow is not fit for Immortals and is utterly useless to any one; a blight never does good to a tree, and if a blight kill not a tree but it still bear fruit, let none say that the fruit was in consequence of the blight."[1]

[1] Letter from Blake to Hayley printed in *The Times Literary Supplement*, July 31, 1930.

IT will be observed that in my frequent references to Plato I for the most part tacitly assume that there is a philosophy of Plato, and that it can be known more or less adequately, as the doctrines of other philosophers are known. I am afraid that, if I do not say something to defend this assumption, I shall be regarded as a belated adherent of a superannuated tradition. However this may be, I can say with truth that I feel equal pleasure in increased insight whether it comes from the traditionary or the revolutionary side. It was with gladness that I saw the return of the world of scholarship to the belief that there was a real Homer; that the *Iliad* and *Odyssey* are not strings of old ballads put together by compilers. On the other hand, the return to acceptance of the "Platonic Epistles" as genuine letters of Plato produces on me the impression of an antithetic error, come in as it were to take the place of an error that has gone.

If I am reminded that I am not a specialist in

[1] See p. 13, note.

philology, I can quote a very drastic passage on the Epistles from a very eminent scholar who is universally recognised as having done one of the most important pieces of philological work on Plato, fixing by definite tests of style the order of the later Dialogues. Lewis Campbell, in an article first published in the ninth edition of the *Encyclopaedia Britannica*, wrote as follows: "The romantic legend of Plato's journeys to Sicily and of his relations there with the younger Dionysius and the princely but unfortunate Dion, had obtained some degree of consistency before the age of Cicero, and at an unknown but probably early time was worked up into the so-called *Epistles* of Plato, now all but universally discredited. Nor is there any sufficient ground for supposing, as some have done, that an authentic tradition is perceptible behind the myth". In the first edition of his *Early Greek Philosophy*, Prof. Burnet evidently took the same view; but since then he and Prof. A. E. Taylor, without reason given, have more and more dogmatically asserted the genuineness of the Epistles, not because any new facts have come to light, but apparently on no ground except the impossibility of distinguishing philologically the kind of Greek in which they are written from the Greek of the *Laws*. On the basis of this acceptance, they have built up a theory of the relations of Plato to Socrates totally incompatible with the tradition usually accepted in letters and in philosophy both in ancient and in modern times.

I hope that the new theory will be subjected to a more searching examination than I can give it from the philological side. My object is merely to show grounds why I may be permitted still to hold that Plato from the beginning to the end of his career was a philosopher, influenced no doubt by others, and above all by Socrates, but never aiming purely and simply at artistic reconstruction of other men's thoughts. To hold this is of course to reject the declaration of the epistolary writer that there never was and never would be a philosophy of Plato.

It is true that Prof. Taylor makes a concession. Plato first set himself to restore the figure and the oral teachings of Socrates; then, when his literary power was to some extent declining, he discovered that he also was something of a philosopher; and from the *Theaetetus* onward there was a new departure. Every one of course perceives certain changes of style between the earlier and the later Dialogues; but in my own case the effect of a recent re-reading was the feeling not of a break but of a profound continuity.

In discussing the "Platonic Apocrypha", Prof. Taylor, in the fourteenth edition of the *Encyclopaedia Britannica*, allows, with only two exceptions, all the exclusions from the list of genuine Dialogues decisively made by the end of the nineteenth century, in addition to those made by the ancients. He proposes to bring back from the modern list of apocryphal writings only the *Epinomis* and the *Epistles*.

Of these the *Epinomis* had already been rejected by Proclus, who was the head of the Academy. This, of course, is not decisive. Proclus himself would not have claimed that it was. There was no unassailable "canon" of the Platonic writings, as I remember that Prof. Taylor himself has pointed out. By a kind of division of labour it was left to the grammarians to bring out the editions. The philosophers read Plato for the matter, and felt free to accept or reject according to their own judgment. Proclus shows himself ready to discuss any question of genuineness. The *Parmenides* having been rejected by some, he defends it not by authority but

on rational grounds. His reason for rejecting the
Epinomis, to any who regard the Neo-Platonists as
simply a school of mystics, will seem paradoxical.
There is too much in it of what we call "theosophy"
for Plato: ἀλλ᾽ ἡ μὲν Ἐπινομὶς νοθείας ὑπάρχουσα
μεστὴ καὶ νοῦ μυστηριώδους τὸν νηπιόφρονα καὶ νῷ
ἀρχαῖον ἀπατᾷ (*Comm. in Remp.* ed. Kroll, II, 134).
And Prof. Dodds has given me a reference to a
passage in the *Platonic Theology* (I, 5, p. 12) in
which, while accepting theosophical formulae
from the Epistles, he passes what seems a rather
depreciatory judgment on them as a source for
knowledge of Plato's doctrine: εἰ δὲ βούλει, κατὰ
τρίτην τάξιν καὶ τὰς ἐπιστολὰς τίθει. Not that this
proves very much; but it suggests, Prof. Dodds
thinks, that they may have been suspect in the
time of Proclus. When the world had returned
again to critical standards, after the long lapse in
which practically no standard of criticism existed,
they soon again became suspect; as is illustrated in
the early eighteenth century, when Anthony Collins, in his *Discourse of Freethinking* (1713), treated
Epistle xiii, which contains a hint of esoteric monotheism, as a Christian forgery. This we know was

wrong; neither monotheism nor triadic speculation, as in Epistle ii, 312 E, was peculiarly Christian; and Bentley, in the reply which he published under the pseudonym of "Phileleutherus Lipsiensis", pointed out that the collection of thirteen Epistles was made up before the beginning of the Christian era. When, however, he taunts Collins with having had more precursors among the learned than he knew, this suggests the thought that doubts shared by several scholars might not be so groundless as Bentley, for his immediate polemical purpose, would have his readers believe.

The most eminent of the recent defenders of the Epistles is Eduard Meyer; who certainly has one very plausible argument: that it is incongruous in historians who treat Ep. vii as an authentic account of events in Plato's life to deny that it was written by Plato. For the ancient writers who preserved the story of Plato at Syracuse had no ultimate source but the Letters. I agree as regards the incongruity; but if there is no other source, and the Letters cannot be confirmed either by external or internal evidence, there seems no alternative but to return to the view at first taken by Burnet, who spoke incidentally, and as if it were a matter of course, of "the romance which passes for Plato's life".[1]

Naturally historians are reluctant to deprive themselves of materials which they have been accustomed to accept; but we are not without all knowledge of Syracusan affairs apart from the "Letters of Plato". In Aristotle's *Politics* there is a much earlier account of the Sicilian revolution than Plutarch's Life of Dion. By Aristotle the case of Dionysius II and Dion is mentioned several times with circumstance; but there is no reference or allusion to any part taken by Plato in the events. Is it likely that the pupil of Plato, who was a member of the Academy at the time, should refer to the relations between Dionysius and Dion without one word about his master's intervention if real?

Is there then internal evidence for the genuineness of the Epistles? Here we come inevitably to subjective impressions; but we need not despair of a consensus, and indeed it once seemed to have been attained. Let us take the case, parallel in many ways, of Shakespeare. The dramatic power in both carries

[1] *Early Greek Philosophy*, 1st ed. p. 301, n. 1.

with it a kind of impersonality, which makes the individual minds of those two among poets and philosophers exceptionally inscrutable. Some plays, however, that were attributed to Shakespeare were treated immediately after his own time as apocryphal, and we have a small list of "Platonic apocrypha" dating from antiquity. The parallel has repeated itself in later criticism. A small list of apocryphal Platonic dialogues has been added to the list that came down to us with the ancient editions; and by this time no critical mind accepts all the contents of the First Folio as equally Shakespearean. There is, besides, considerable agreement as to what is non-Shakespearean.

We need not shrink, then, from examining critically the story about Plato and the Letters attributed to him. Do we find them worthy of Plato's mind and character as reasonably inferred from the Dialogues? I can only say that I do not. By some, however, we seem to be expected to believe that Plato thought an episode of futile action, for which it was necessary to accept partial dependence on a despot, a greater thing than to have written the *Republic*; and Prof. Taylor apparently thinks that the figure of Socrates would gain dignity if it could be proved that he might have described himself, like Dogberry, as "a fellow that hath had losses".

A source for the romance of Plato and Dionysius can be very plausibly assigned. I do not take any of the "Platonic apocrypha" to have been forgeries sold to the Academy. The apocryphal Dialogues were probably exercises written in the Academy, preserved for some special merit, and not at first carefully marked off from Plato's own writing. The Epistles I can understand as experiments in fiction by a reader of the *Laws*, if they were suggested by a passage in which the "Athenian Stranger" argues that a favourable condition for bringing into action a new system of legislation would be that the ideas of a great legislator should be taken up by a young and vigorous despot. As Dion may have been a pupil of Plato, and was certainly, we may gather even from Aristotle's brief account, what would now be called a political "idealist", the writer set himself to work out the consequences of bringing Plato directly into the Sicilian revolution. Since the fact of Dion's ultimate failure was known, the

intervention of the philosopher could not be represented as successful; but for the spirit of the next age
the failure could be turned to honour. If we place
the composition of the Letters within about twenty
years after the almost simultaneous deaths of Alexander and of Aristotle, then they appealed to an age
of returning monarchy; and any slight objection
that might be felt to Plato's addressing Dionysius as
in some sense his patron would be quite obviated
by his rigorous pedantry in refusing to let the
young despot begin to reform the State till he had
been adequately instructed in geometry. To us
Dionysius seems to have fair reason for complaint;
but the conventional character of the philosopher
had to be preserved. This was now to be presented
in a new light. To outsiders it had long been a topic
of ridicule; as when Strepsiades in the *Clouds* remon-
strates with Socrates for insisting on teaching him
the elements of grammar and rhythm, which he
could not see to have any bearing on the definite
practical purpose of not paying his creditors. In the
new era of professional philosophy the impractic-
ability was transformed into a ground of pride. The
philosopher fails through his virtues.

There is no sign, however, that Plato's school ever took much interest in his supposed adventures. The Epistles were allowed to pass for Plato's, but nothing was founded on them. So far was philosophical and literary tradition from the naïve treatment of Plato as a dresser-up of his master's sayings that probably too little importance was attached to the personality of Socrates, to whose conversational method we owe Plato as a literary artist, just as we owe Shakespeare to the preparation of the dramatic form appropriate to his genius by the earlier Elizabethans.

No one, of course, will deny that in detail Platonic criticism owes a great deal to Professors Burnet and Taylor. In particular, the perfectly established distinction (lost before the time of Proclus) between the Critias of the *Timaeus* (with its sequel) and his grandson the member of the Thirty (who appears in the *Charmides* and the *Protagoras*) clears up many things that were obscure.[1] I have no doubt that Burnet was right in his expression of the opinion that most of the poetical fragments ascribed to the

[1] But for the preservation of the facts by Alexander of Aphrodisias (vaguely referred to by Philoponus as cited by Diels, *Fragmente der Vorsokratiker*, II, i, 2nd ed. p. 612), the notoriety of the younger would have effaced all memory of the elder Critias, Plato's great-grandfather.

younger Critias are really his grandfather's. I had
never been able to succeed in finding different
aspects of the same personality in the elegiac fragments and in the vehement and aggressive speech preserved by Sextus Empiricus from the satyric drama
called the *Sisyphus*, arguing that the invention of
"the race of gods" was a device of statesmen. But
no more can I reconcile the author of the Dialogues
with the representation of Plato in the Epistles.

   This is not to say that no facts whatever about
Plato were turned to account in the Letters, *e.g.*, in the
seventh. From what we know authentically about
his family, we might be sure, even if we had not
been told, that he was offered a political opening by
the Thirty (in whom were included his near relations Charmides and Critias) and that he declined
it. If he had not declined it, there would certainly
never have been any philosophy of Plato; but I
cannot believe that Plato seriously wrote that there
was actually no such thing; though it is possible
that in conversation, like other writers of dialogues,
he may have occasionally protested that the opinions
expressed by his personages, even by Socrates, were
not necessarily to be taken for his own.

If we are to do justice to the real ability of the epistolary writer, we must, as far as possible, get out of our heads the controversial question whether he may not have been Plato, and treat the whole as a romance founded on a legend. Of the legend of Plato's intervention at Syracuse, so far as I know, there is not a trace in what has been preserved from historical writers between the ages of Plato and of Cicero. The author, however, had a definite conception of Plato which he desired to communicate; and he had assimilated the style of the *Laws*, from which he borrows most frequently though not exclusively. The greatest master of the expression of thought in prose who ever lived had himself, in a well-known passage near the end of the *Phaedrus*, dwelt on the limitations of written language. In a less generally known passage of the *Laws* (xii, 968 B–E) he had described great thoughts as best developed by long meditation and oral interchange. Now in the often-quoted passage from Epistle vii (341 C, D), describing the sudden bursting forth of insight into flame as of a self-nourished fire in the soul, the author has given condensed and powerful expression, in Platonic terms, to a real psychological observation; but unfortunately (as it seems to me in view of the consequences) he has interpreted Plato's recognition of the limits of discursive reasoning and written expression as a serious intention never to write a treatise of his own on philosophy. Thus the philosopher has come to be represented as a mystagogue, determined to make no attempt to convey his deeper convictions to the public, but giving an occasional hint to a fit hearer like Dionysius; of whose claims, however, to have had original thoughts of his own on philosophy, or even to have rapidly understood what his teacher meant, Plato is made to show himself somewhat jealous. Now, as the *Timaeus* was undoubtedly a published treatise of Plato of an abstruse kind, the modern accepters of the Epistles must needs try to make out that in the *Timaeus* Plato did not mean to expound his own analysis of the elements of the world even in mythical form. There has followed a kind of repetition of what took place in antiquity. An unknown writer, whose work we still possess, wrote a brief exposition of the *Timaeus* in Doric, entitled Περὶ ψυχᾶς κόσμω καὶ φύσιος. This was ascribed to the actual Timaeus (of whom, it is agreed, we know nothing) who sets forth the myth of creation in the Platonic dialogue; and Plato's ancient successors—finding in it a useful summary, as in fact it is—took it to be a genuine work of Timaeus of Locri. In the modern theory, which I understand to be that of Prof. Taylor's Commentary (1928), it seems to be inferred that, since the "Plato" of the Epistles said that he would not write any treatise of his own on such subjects, Plato in his actual treatise was simply trying to reconstruct what might have been the theory of a South Italian Pythagorean of the fifth century. On the whole, the ancient ascription of an original treatise to "Timaeus Locrus" from which Plato borrowed, though it has by general consent been abandoned and I do not accept it, seems to me more plausible.

INDEX

Aeschylus, 17

Agnosticism, philosophical tradition of, 49–51

Alexander of Aphrodisias, 112 n.

"Animal Automatism", 87

Aristophanes, 20; the *Clouds* glanced at, 111

Aristotle, 9, 12, 13, 15, 17, 18, 23, 26, 32, 34, 36, 57, 74 n., 85 n., 89, 90, 91, 92, 95, 108, 110, 111

Arnold, M. (quoted), 78

"Association of Ideas", A. Bain on, 7 n.; in Plato and Aristotle, 23; in English psychology, in the German school of J. F. Herbart, and in F. H. Bradley, 36–7

Babylonia, beginnings of science in, 10

Bacon, induction as conceived by, 2; 27, 29, 70

Bain, A., on limitation of voluntarist psychology, 7 n.

"Behaviourism", 88

Bentley, R., 107

Bergson, H., 91

Berkeley, 39, 40, 41, 42, 44, 45

Blake, W., 101

Bradley, F. H., 36, 37, 52, 68

Bruno, Giordano, 56

Burnet, J., 11, 74, 103 ff.

Campbell, L., 103

Cicero, 103, 114

Coleridge, S. T., 20

Collins, Anthony, 106, 107

Comte, A., 33, 34, 35, 46, 48, 70, 72, 83

Critias, the elder and the younger in Platonic dialogues, 112, 113

Cusa, Nicholas of, 55, 56, 82

Damascius, 50

Dante, 59

Democracy, Athenian, and philosophy, 16–17

Democritus, 42, 46

Descartes, 26, 27, 28, 33, 39, 56, 70

Determinism, 95–100

Dodds, E. R., 51 n., 106

Eddington, Sir A. S., 46, 47, 63, 81

Egypt, beginnings of science in, 9

Einstein, A., 66, 67

Epicureanism, naturalistic system, 23

Epicurus, 42; his indeterminism, 95

Erigena, John Scotus, 81

For EU product safety concerns, contact us at Calle de José Abascal, 56–1°,
28003 Madrid, Spain or eugpsr@cambridge.org.

www.ingramcontent.com/pod-product-compliance
Ingram Content Group UK Ltd.
Pitfield, Milton Keynes, MK11 3LW, UK
UKHW020313140625

459647UK00018B/1849